PAT BROWN, MBA

BaseballMoney101

Using Baseball to Teach the Basics of Money

ABRAM 47 BROWN

First published by AbramBrown47 2026

First edition

ISBN: 978-1-967737-62-8

This book was professionally typeset on Reedsy.
Find out more at reedsy.com

Contents

Foreword

Playing the Long Game

Baseball teaches you something early that most sports do not.

You can do everything right and still fail.

You can square up the ball and line it straight at someone. You can throw a perfect pitch and watch it get blooped for a hit. You can prepare all week, execute the plan, and still walk back to the dugout 0-for-4. In baseball, failure is not an exception. It is part of the job.

That reality shapes players in ways that last long after the final out.

Baseball is a game of patience. A game of repetition. A game where small advantages matter more than big moments. You win over time, not all at once. You stay in the lineup by showing up every day, doing your job, and trusting that the work will show up eventually.

Money works the same way.

This book exists because too many athletes leave the game without realizing that the mindset baseball taught them is exactly the mindset required to win financially. The problem is not effort. Athletes work harder than almost anyone. The problem is translation. Nobody ever sits players down and explains how the discipline, patience, and long-game thinking they learned between the lines applies to money once the season ends.

So athletes improvise.

They guess.

They copy what they hear in clubhouses.

They chase quick wins.

They panic during slumps.

And just like baseball, those habits get exposed over time.

Baseball Money 101 is not about turning athletes into finance experts. It is about giving them a familiar language for unfamiliar decisions. It is about showing players that the same approach that keeps you in the lineup for a long season can keep you financially stable for a long life.

This book was written by someone who understands locker rooms, pressure, and accountability.

Pat Brown played college football at the University of Kansas from 1994 to 1999 and was named team captain his senior season. He knows what it means to earn trust, prepare every day, and lead when things are not going well. While football and baseball are different games, the cultures overlap in important ways. Both demand discipline. Both expose shortcuts. Both reward consistency far more than flash.

After football, Pat transitioned into financial services and built a career working with individuals, families, business owners, and athletes navigating increasingly complex financial lives. Over the years, he saw a pattern that kept repeating. Athletes were not failing financially because they were reckless or lazy. They were failing because nobody ever handed them a playbook.

They had talent.

They had work ethic.

They had confidence.

What they lacked was structure.

As the college sports landscape changed with Name, Image, and Likeness opportunities, that gap became even more obvious. Young athletes were suddenly earning income, signing contracts, and making tax-sensitive decisions without understanding cash flow, risk, or long-term consequences. The game sped up, but the education never arrived.

Baseball Money 101 is part of Pat's response to that gap.

This book does not promise shortcuts. It does not sell hype. It does not pretend money is easy or predictable. Instead, it respects the intelligence of athletes and speaks to them the way coaches do. Directly. Honestly. With an emphasis on fundamentals.

If you played baseball, much of what you read here will feel familiar.

You will see money framed like a season, not a single game.

You will see budgeting treated like small ball, not punishment.

You will see investing compared to staying in the lineup, not swinging for the fences every at-bat.

You will see risk described the way pitchers think about counts, not bravado.

That is intentional.

Baseball rewards players who understand context. The count matters. The situation matters. The inning matters. The season matters. Trying to play every at-bat the same way is how careers end early.

Money punishes the same mistake.

Too many people approach finances as if every decision needs to be aggressive. Maximize returns. Leverage everything. Move fast. Take big swings. That approach looks exciting in highlights. Over a full season, it leads to strikeouts, injuries, and time on the bench.

Baseball Money 101 is about staying in the game.

It is about learning when to swing and when to take a pitch.

It is about understanding that walks matter.

It is about respecting defense, protection, and fundamentals.

It is about knowing that consistency beats intensity.

This book also understands something baseball players know well. Your career on the field is short. Your career off the field is long. The habits you build now will either compound quietly in your favor or work against you when you least expect it.

You do not need to be perfect to win financially. Baseball proves that every day. You need to stay composed during slumps. You need to avoid chasing bad pitches. You need to trust the process even when the results lag behind the effort.

Most importantly, you need to stop thinking of money as something separate from who you are as an athlete.

The discipline that got you here still matters.

The preparation still matters.

The mindset still matters.

What changes is the scoreboard.

This book is an invitation to see money the way baseball teaches you to see the game. One rep at a time. One decision at a time. One season at a time.

If you commit to that approach, you do not need a miracle swing. You need patience, awareness, and the willingness to play the long game.

That is how careers last.

That is how wealth is built.

That is how you stay in the lineup long after the uniform comes off.

Introduction

The Season Is Long and So Is Your Financial Life

Every baseball player learns this lesson sooner or later.

You do not win a season in April.

You do not lose a season in April either.

The standings in the first few weeks rarely tell the real story. Teams are still finding their rhythm. Pitchers are building arm strength. Hitters are adjusting timing. Slumps come early. So do hot streaks. The players who survive are not the ones who panic after a bad series or get arrogant after a good one. They are the ones who understand the season is long.

Money works the same way.

Most financial mistakes happen because people treat money like a single game instead of a full season. They overreact to short-term results. They chase hot streaks. They abandon the plan after a slump. They make emotional decisions because they forget that progress in life, like progress in baseball, is uneven.

This book exists to reset that perspective.

If you played baseball, you already understand the mindset required to win financially. What you may not realize is how directly those lessons apply once the cleats come off. The problem is not that athletes lack discipline. It is that no one ever connects the dots.

Why Money Feels Harder Than Baseball

Baseball is difficult, but it is not confusing.

The rules are clear. The scoreboard is visible. The feedback is immediate. You know when you missed a pitch. You know when you made an error. You know where you stand in the lineup.

Money does not give feedback that cleanly.

Bills arrive at different times. Income changes. Decisions made years ago show up today. Some mistakes feel painless at first and devastating later. Others feel uncomfortable early and rewarding over time. Without a system, it is easy to feel lost.

That is why so many athletes say money feels harder than the game they played.

It is not because money is more complex. It is because money is less structured.

During your playing career, structure was everywhere. Practice times were set. Strength programs were designed for you. Coaches watched film. Trainers monitored recovery. Even meals and travel were handled.

Then one day, the season ends.

No schedule.

No staff.

No daily accountability.

You are expected to manage income, expenses, taxes, insurance, investing, and long-term planning without reps, film, or coaching. That transition hits harder than most people admit.

This book is designed to replace some of that missing structure.

The Baseball Advantage You Already Have

Baseball quietly teaches traits that matter deeply in financial life.

Patience.

Resilience.

Emotional control.

Long-term thinking.

A .300 hitter fails seven out of ten times. A closer blows saves. A Cy Young winner gives up home runs. Baseball forces you to detach ego from outcome and focus on process.

That mindset is rare outside of sports. It is also exactly what money requires.

Financial success is not about being right all the time. It is about staying disciplined when results are uneven. It is about avoiding panic during slumps and avoiding arrogance during hot streaks. It is about trusting the fundamentals even when the scoreboard lags.

If you learned how to handle failure in baseball, you already have an edge.

Why This Book Is Not About Getting Rich Fast

There are plenty of books that promise shortcuts.

They talk about hacks, secrets, and strategies that sound exciting. They appeal to urgency and fear. They imply that if you are not doing something aggressive right now, you are falling behind.

Baseball teaches you to be skeptical of that mindset.

No one builds a career on miracle swings. No one stays in the league by chasing highlights. The players who last are the ones who understand situational hitting, defensive positioning, and preparation.

This book takes the same approach.

Baseball Money 101 is not about maximizing returns at all costs. It is about building a financial system that holds up over decades. It is about defense as much as offense. Protection as much as growth. Consistency over intensity.

You will see themes repeated throughout this book because repetition matters. Just like in baseball, fundamentals are reinforced daily because they break down under pressure.

Money Is a Season, Not a Series

One of the biggest mistakes people make is judging financial progress too quickly.

A bad month feels like failure.

A good month feels like success.

Neither tells the full story.

In baseball, you zoom out. You look at trends. You track performance over time. You trust the sample size. You know that small slumps are part of the process.

Money deserves the same patience.

This book will repeatedly bring you back to one idea. You are not trying to win today. You are trying to stay in the game.

That mindset changes everything.

It changes how you think about saving.

It changes how you think about debt.

It changes how you think about risk.

It changes how you react to mistakes.

Instead of asking, "Did this work immediately?" you start asking, "Does this hold up over time?"

The Cost of Playing Without a Game Plan

No team shows up to the park without a plan.

You may adjust lineups. You may change pitching strategy. You may adapt to weather and matchups. But you never walk out and hope talent carries you.

Financially, many people do exactly that.

They earn money and assume things will work out. They react to expenses instead of planning for them. They save when convenient. They invest when excited. They borrow when pressured.

That approach feels fine early. Just like raw talent feels fine in youth baseball. Over time, the gaps get exposed.

This book is your playbook.

Not a rigid script, but a framework. A way to think through decisions using concepts you already understand. Every chapter connects money back to the sport so that the lessons stick under pressure.

Why Defense Matters More Than You Think

Baseball fans love offense.

Home runs. Big innings. Walk-off hits.

But players know defense keeps you employed.

Missed assignments cost games. Poor fundamentals extend innings. Lack of protection wears teams down over a long season.

Financially, defense is often ignored.

Emergency funds. Insurance. Risk management. These topics do not feel exciting. They also prevent seasons from ending early.

This book spends significant time on protection because that is what keeps you available. You cannot build wealth if one setback wipes you out. You cannot invest confidently if you are constantly exposed.

Defense is not fear. It is discipline.

Adjustments Are Part of the Game

No baseball season goes exactly as planned.

Injuries happen. Roles change. Careers take unexpected turns. Opportunities appear. Others disappear.

Money works the same way.

Your income will change. Your priorities will shift. Your responsibilities will grow. The plan must adapt without falling apart.

This book emphasizes adjustment over perfection.

You will learn when to hold steady.

When to rebalance.

When to simplify.

When to protect.

Just like baseball, the goal is not to avoid mistakes. The goal is to respond correctly when they happen.

Who This Book Is For

This book is written for current and former baseball players.

High school athletes.

College athletes.

Former professionals.

Lifelong competitors.

You do not need a finance background. You do not need perfect habits. You do not need to have everything figured out.

You need willingness.

Willingness to be honest.

Willingness to learn.

Willingness to treat money with the same respect you gave the game.

The Big Idea You Will See Repeated

Everything in this book comes back to one principle.

Consistency beats intensity.

In baseball, that truth is obvious. In money, it is often ignored.

You do not need one big swing.

You need a thousand good at-bats.

You do not need perfect timing.

You need discipline over time.

You do not need to be fearless.

You need to be prepared.

What Comes Next

The chapters that follow are organized like a season.

You will start with fundamentals.

You will build protection.

You will learn offense.

You will make adjustments.

You will prepare for life after the game.

Each chapter stands on its own, but together they form a system.

This is not about turning you into someone else. It is about helping you use the mindset you already earned through baseball to build a financial life that lasts.

The season is long.

So is your financial life.

The goal is not to win early.

The goal is to still be standing at the end.

About This Book

What Baseball Teaches Us About Money

Baseball is a thinking person's game.

From the outside, it can look slow or simple. From the inside, it is layered with nuance. Pitch sequencing. Situational hitting. Defensive positioning. Managing fatigue. Reading tendencies. Adjusting over time. Baseball rewards players who can think long-term while staying locked into the present moment.

Money works the same way.

At first glance, finances seem straightforward. Earn money. Pay bills. Save what is left. Invest when you can. But once real life enters the picture, the game changes. Income fluctuates. Expenses surprise you. Emotions show up. Long-term decisions compete with short-term pressure. Without a framework, it is easy to feel like you are guessing.

This book exists to give you that framework using a language you already understand.

Baseball Is a Long-Game Sport

Unlike many sports, baseball does not reward impatience.

You can do everything right and still fail today. You can do something wrong and get lucky. The sport forces you to separate outcome from process. A well-hit ball can be an out. A bloop can be a hit. Over time, the process wins.

Money behaves the same way.

A good financial decision does not always feel good immediately. Saving money can feel restrictive. Paying down debt can feel slow. Staying invested during market swings can feel uncomfortable. On the other hand, bad financial decisions often feel great at first. Spending is fun. Risk feels exciting. Shortcuts look efficient.

Baseball teaches you to judge success over seasons, not innings. This book asks you to apply that same patience to your financial life.

Fundamentals Win Championships and Build Wealth

Every great baseball program obsesses over fundamentals.

Throwing mechanics. Footwork. Balance. Plate discipline. Situational awareness. These are not glamorous skills, but they show up every day. When pressure increases, fundamentals either hold or break.

Money has fundamentals too.

Cash flow.

Budgeting.

Emergency savings.

Risk management.

Long-term investing discipline.

Most financial stress comes from skipping these basics. People jump straight to advanced strategies, just like a player trying to hit home runs before learning how to make contact. This book starts with fundamentals on purpose.

Not because fundamentals are boring, but because they are reliable.

Process Over Highlights

Baseball culture quietly teaches humility.

Even the best players in the world make outs most of the time. No one expects perfection. What coaches expect is effort, preparation, and consistency. You earn trust by doing the little things right over and over.

Financial culture often pushes the opposite message.

Big wins are celebrated. Quiet discipline is ignored. People talk about returns, not risk. They share success stories, not close calls. This creates pressure to swing for the fences financially, even when the situation calls for a single.

This book pushes back on that mindset.

We focus on process.

We emphasize consistency.

We respect defense.

Because that is how baseball works, and that is how money works.

Failure Is Part of the System

Baseball normalizes failure in a way few environments do.

Strikeouts happen. Errors happen. Slumps happen. The response matters more than the mistake. Players who spiral after failure do not last. Players who adjust do.

Money demands the same emotional maturity.

You will overspend sometimes.

You will make decisions you wish you had handled differently.

You will miss opportunities.

This book does not assume perfection. It assumes you are human.

Instead of asking how to avoid mistakes entirely, we focus on how to recover quickly and prevent small issues from becoming season-ending problems. Baseball teaches you to move on to the next pitch. Financial discipline requires the same skill.

Defense Is Not Optional

Fans love offense.

Home runs. Big innings. Walk-offs.

Players know defense keeps you on the field.

Strong fundamentals prevent errors from compounding. Good positioning limits damage. Smart decisions protect leads. Over a long season, defense saves arms, protects confidence, and keeps teams competitive.

Financial defense is often ignored.

Emergency funds.

Insurance.

Risk awareness.

Liquidity.

These topics do not feel exciting, but they prevent financial injuries. This book treats protection as a core part of winning, not an afterthought. You cannot build wealth if one unexpected event knocks you out of the game.

Adjustments Matter More Than Ego

No baseball season goes according to plan.

Lineups change. Roles evolve. Players get injured. New opportunities appear. The teams that survive are the ones that adjust without panic and without ego.

Money requires the same flexibility.

What worked in your twenties may not work in your forties. Income changes. Family responsibilities grow. Risk tolerance shifts. This book emphasizes adjustment over rigidity.

The goal is not to lock into one perfect strategy. The goal is to build a system that can adapt as your life changes.

Why Analogies Work

Sports analogies are not used here to oversimplify money. They are used to make it stick.

You already understand reps, seasons, slumps, pressure, and preparation. When financial concepts are framed through baseball, they stop feeling abstract. They become practical. They become familiar.

This book consistently connects money decisions back to the game so that lessons hold up when emotions show up. Just like on the field, execution matters most when pressure is high.

Who This Book Is Written For

This book is written for current and former baseball players.

It assumes you understand discipline.

It assumes you respect coaching.

It assumes you know what it feels like to prepare, fail, adjust, and try again.

You do not need financial expertise. You need willingness to apply what you already know from baseball to a different arena.

The Core Philosophy

One idea runs through every chapter.

You do not need to be perfect.

You need to be consistent.

Baseball Money 101 is not about turning you into a financial expert. It is about helping you play the long game with confidence, discipline, and control.

Just like baseball.

The game rewards those who respect it.

Money does too.

Foolish Assumptions

What This Book Assumes About You as a Player and a Person

Every good coach starts with assumptions.

Not about talent. Not about outcomes. About effort, mindset, and responsibility. Coaches assume certain things about the people in the locker room because without shared expectations, nothing works. The system breaks down. Accountability disappears. Progress stalls.

This section does the same thing.

Before we talk about money, strategy, or long-term planning, we need to be clear about what this book assumes about you. These are not flattering assumptions or critical ones. They are practical. They are honest. And they are necessary for everything else in this book to make sense.

If these assumptions do not fit you, that is not a judgment. It simply means this book may not land the way it is intended to.

Assumption #1: You Are Used to Being Coached Hard

This book assumes you have been coached.

Not motivational quotes and vague encouragement. Real coaching. Correction. Accountability. Film sessions that pointed out mistakes. Reps that exposed weaknesses. Standards that were non-negotiable.

Baseball players understand this environment.

You have been told to fix your footwork.

You have been challenged on your preparation.

You have been benched, adjusted, or pushed because performance mattered.

This book uses that same tone.

It will not sugarcoat.

It will not hype shortcuts.

It will not pretend that effort alone fixes everything.

Money, like baseball, responds to structure and discipline, not feelings. If you are comfortable being coached and challenged, this book will feel familiar. If you expect validation without accountability, it may feel uncomfortable.

That discomfort is part of growth.

Assumption #2: You Understand That Fundamentals Matter More Than Talent

Every baseball player has seen talent fail.

The kid with the best swing who never adjusted.

The pitcher with elite velocity who never learned control.

The athlete who relied on ability instead of preparation.

You already know that talent opens doors, but habits keep you in the game.

This book assumes you believe the same thing applies to money.

You do not need to be brilliant.

You do not need insider knowledge.

You do not need perfect timing.

You need fundamentals.

Cash flow awareness.

Basic budgeting.

Saving consistently.

Managing risk.

Staying disciplined when emotions rise.

If you believe fundamentals are beneath you, this book will frustrate you. If you believe fundamentals win championships and careers, this book will feel practical and empowering.

Assumption #3: You Know the Difference Between Effort and Execution

Baseball teaches a hard truth early.

Trying hard is not the same as executing well.

You can work your tail off and still miss a cutoff.

You can prepare and still miss a sign.

You can hustle and still make a poor decision.

This book assumes you understand that money works the same way.

Good intentions do not replace systems.

Effort does not replace planning.

Motivation does not replace consistency.

Saying "I'm trying" does not change outcomes in baseball. It does not change outcomes financially either. This book focuses on execution because execution is what moves results.

Assumption #4: You Accept Responsibility for Outcomes

Umpires miss calls.

Weather changes games.

Teammates make mistakes.

Great players still take responsibility.

They control what they can control.

They adjust.

They move on.

This book assumes you are willing to take responsibility for your financial outcomes, even when circumstances are not perfect.

That does not mean blaming yourself for everything.

It means not outsourcing responsibility.

Not blaming schools for not teaching you.

Not blaming coaches for focusing on performance.

Not blaming parents, advisors, or timing.

You may not have been given a financial playbook early. That is real. But once you recognize the gap, responsibility becomes yours. This book exists to close that gap, not to assign blame.

Assumption #5: You Are Willing to Play the Long Game

Baseball rewards patience in a way few sports do.

You cannot force a season into a week.

You cannot judge a hitter on one at-bat.

You cannot panic after one bad series.

This book assumes you are willing to apply that same patience to money.

No get-rich-quick mindset.

No obsession with short-term wins.

No comparing your Chapter 3 to someone else's Chapter 15.

If you want immediate results and constant excitement, money will frustrate you. If you understand that progress compounds quietly, this book will make sense.

Assumption #6: You Know That Boring Usually Means Working

Conditioning is boring.

Long toss is boring.

Fundamental drills are boring.

They work anyway.

This book assumes you are willing to do unglamorous financial work.

Looking at bank statements.

Setting up automatic savings.

Reading insurance policies.

Understanding debt before using it.

None of this feels exciting. All of it prevents future problems.

If you expect money to feel thrilling all the time, you will make mistakes. If you are comfortable with boring work that produces results, you are in the right place.

Assumption #7: You Have Felt the Identity Shift After the Game

This is an important one.

This book assumes you are more than just a player, but that being a player shaped you.

Whether your career ended recently or years ago, baseball structured your life. When that structure changes, many athletes feel unprepared in areas that had nothing to do with performance.

Money is one of those areas.

This book assumes you want to build an identity that includes, but is not limited to, your time in uniform. Financial confidence is part of that next chapter.

Assumption #8: You Want Control, Not Perfection

Baseball humbles anyone chasing perfection.

The best hitters fail most of the time.

The best pitchers give up runs.

The best teams lose games.

This book assumes you are not chasing perfect financial decisions. You are chasing control.

Control of cash flow.

Control of risk.

Control of choices.

Control creates confidence. Confidence allows patience. Patience produces long-term success.

Why These Assumptions Matter

If these assumptions hold true, this book will feel like a coach you trust.

Direct.

Practical.

Honest.

Focused on fundamentals.

If they do not, the lessons may feel repetitive or uncomfortable. That does not mean they are wrong. It means they require a mindset shift.

Baseball taught you how to prepare, compete, fail, adjust, and try again. This book assumes you are willing to apply those same skills to money.

Because money, like baseball, is not about one play.

It is about showing up, staying disciplined, and playing the season the right way.

Final Thought

No coach assumes perfection.

They assume effort, accountability, and willingness to learn.

That is all this book assumes of you.

If you bring that mindset, the rest will follow.

How This Playbook Is Organized

Every good baseball season follows a rhythm.

You do not start Opening Day with playoff strategies. You do not work on late-season adjustments before spring training. You build in layers. Fundamentals first. Then protection. Then strategy. Then adjustment. Then life after the game.

This book is organized the same way.

It is not meant to be read like a textbook. It is meant to be used like a playbook. You can read it cover to cover, or you can jump to the section that matches where you are right now. Either way, the structure matters, because each part builds on the one before it.

Think of this book as a full season, not a single series.

Front Matter: Setting the Tone

The opening sections exist to set expectations and mindset.

The foreword, introduction, and early framing are not about tactics. They are about perspective. They explain why money feels different once the uniform comes off, why so many athletes feel behind even when they are capable, and why a long-term approach matters.

This is where the mental shift begins.

Before mechanics matter, mindset matters. Baseball taught you that. Money works the same way.

Part I: Spring Training and Fundamentals

This is where everything starts.

Spring training is not about standings. It is about habits. Timing. Reps. Getting comfortable with basics before pressure counts.

Part I focuses on financial fundamentals:

Understanding why money feels confusing after sports

Learning to read your financial box score

Building simple budgeting and saving systems

Understanding credit and debt

Organizing your banking system

This section is intentionally practical and repetitive. That is not an accident.

Just like baseball fundamentals, these concepts are simple but not easy. Many athletes skip them because they feel basic. That mistake shows up later in the season when pressure increases.

If you only read one part of this book, make it this one.

Part II: Defense and Protection

You cannot win games if you cannot protect a lead.

This section focuses on risk awareness and insurance. Topics that athletes often ignore because nothing bad has happened yet.

Part II covers:

Understanding risk beyond emotion

Health, auto, renters, and homeowners insurance

Life, disability, and liability coverage

Why protection keeps you available

This is the defensive side of money. It is not exciting. It is essential.

Strong teams respect defense. Strong financial lives do too.

Part III: Offense and Growth

Once the foundation and protection are in place, you can focus on growth.

This section introduces investing concepts through baseball language and structure. It explains how markets work, what stocks and bonds actually represent, and how team-based investing reduces mistakes.

Topics include:

Stocks and ownership

Bonds as defense

Funds and ETFs

Real estate and alternatives

This section is not about hype or predictions. It is about understanding roles. Just like a lineup, each investment type serves a purpose. When roles are misunderstood, performance suffers.

Part IV: Managing the Season

Every long season requires adjustments.

This part focuses on maintaining balance and discipline over time. It explains how to build an investment lineup, how to trust the process during volatility, and how to rebalance without overreacting.

Key themes include:

Asset allocation

Buy-and-hold discipline

Rebalancing

The mental game of money

This is where many people fail, not because they lack knowledge, but because they abandon the plan when pressure hits. Baseball prepares you for slumps. This section shows you how to handle financial ones.

Part V: The Long Career and Life After Baseball

Baseball ends for everyone.

This part focuses on life beyond the game. Taxes, retirement, housing decisions, career transitions, estate planning, and family conversations all show up here.

Topics include:

Taxes and account placement

Retirement planning

Big financial decisions

Career and income strategy

Estate planning basics

Family communication

This section recognizes that financial success is not just about numbers. It is about people, transitions, and responsibility.

Part VI: Staying in the Game

The final section brings everything together.

It focuses on advisors, scams, common mistakes, and long-term rules for success. This is about sustainability.

Knowing when to ask for help

Recognizing bad advice

Avoiding shortcuts

Playing the long game

This section reinforces a simple truth. The goal is not to be perfect. The goal is to stay in the game long after the final inning.

How to Use This Book

You can use this book in three ways.

First, you can read it straight through like a season. That builds context and confidence.

Second, you can jump to the part that matches your current situation. Just like a coach adjusting a game plan mid-season.

Third, you can revisit chapters over time. Financial understanding changes as life changes. What matters at twenty-two is different at thirty-five.

There is no wrong way to use this playbook, as long as you use it.

Final Thought

Baseball teaches patience, discipline, and respect for the process.

This book is organized to reflect that reality.

No shortcuts.

No gimmicks.

No hero ball.

Just fundamentals, protection, growth, adjustment, and long-term success.

Play the season the right way, and the results take care of themselves.

About Pat Brown

Pat Brown understands the long game because he lived it.

Long before he worked in financial services, Pat learned about discipline, accountability, preparation, and pressure inside a locker room. He played college football at the University of Kansas from 1994 to 1999 and was named team captain for the 1999 season. Those years were not just about wins and losses. They were about showing up every day, earning trust, competing through adversity, and learning that consistency matters more than flash.

Football shaped how Pat thinks.

It taught him that effort is non-negotiable. That preparation shows up when pressure hits. That the scoreboard does not care how you feel. And that leadership is about responsibility, not recognition. Those lessons did not stop mattering when his playing career ended. They became the foundation for everything that came next.

From the Locker Room to Financial Services

Like every athlete, Pat eventually faced the transition out of sports.

The structure disappeared. The schedule changed. The accountability shifted. Suddenly, performance was no longer measured by film sessions and game stats, but by decisions made quietly and consistently over time. Money became one of those decisions.

Pat transitioned into the financial services industry and built a career as a financial advisor and wealth manager. He works with individuals, families, business owners, and athletes who are navigating increasingly complex financial lives. Over the years, he saw a pattern repeat itself.

Smart, disciplined people struggled with money not because they lacked intelligence or work ethic, but because they lacked a system.

They had never been given a playbook.

Education Meets Real-World Experience

Pat believed athletes deserved better preparation than trial and error.

To deepen his expertise, he pursued advanced education and professional development, earning his MBA along with industry designations including ChFC®, RICP®, and CAP®. His work spans comprehensive financial planning, retirement income strategies, tax planning, and philanthropy. He blends technical knowledge with real-world experience, focusing on practical decisions rather than theory.

But credentials were never the point.

The point was translating complexity into clarity, especially for people who had been coached hard in sports but never coached in money.

The NIL Wake-Up Call

When the college sports landscape changed with the introduction of Name, Image, and Likeness opportunities, Pat saw the education gap widen overnight.

Student-athletes were gaining access to income, contracts, endorsements, and business opportunities without the financial knowledge needed to manage taxes, cash flow, legal structures, and long-term consequences. The pressure to monetize came fast. The education came late.

That reality became a turning point.

Pat began working extensively in the NIL space, helping athletes and families understand what money actually does to decision-making, relationships, and long-term outcomes. He became a recognized voice in athlete financial education and has been interviewed by national publications and platforms including *Financial Planning*, *Yahoo*, and *ESPN Andscape*, where he shares insights on NIL planning, financial literacy gaps, and the challenges facing student-athletes and their families.

Writing the Playbook Athletes Never Got

These experiences led Pat to write.

Not academic books.

Not theory-heavy manuals.

Practical playbooks written in athlete language.

His NIL-focused titles include:

Financial Literacy for NIL

Financial Literacy for NIL for Parents of Student Athletes

Financial Literacy for NIL for High School Students

Financial Literacy for NIL for International Student Athletes

Each book is designed to meet athletes and families where they are, using real scenarios instead of hypotheticals and structure instead of fear.

From there, the vision expanded.

Pat created a growing collection of sport-specific financial education titles, including:

Football Money 101

Baseball Money 101

Basketball Money 101

Cheer Money 101

Dance Money 101

Gymnastics Money 101

Hockey Money 101

Lacrosse Money 101

Rowing Money 101

Soccer Money 101

Softball Money 101

Tennis Money 101

Track Money 101

Volleyball Money 101

Wrestling Money 101

Each book translates the culture, discipline, and mindset of the sport into financial lessons athletes can apply long after competition ends.

Former Student Athlete

Writing books was only part of the mission.

To extend this work beyond the page, Pat founded **Former Student Athlete**, a platform created to support athletes navigating life after sports. Former Student Athlete focuses on education, community, and real-world resources related to financial literacy, career transitions, health, identity, and long-term success once the uniform comes off.

You can explore this work at:

www.formerstudentathlete.com

www.financialliteracyfornil.com

www.financialliteracyforstudentathletes.com

The platform reflects Pat's core belief: athletes should not have to figure out life after sports alone.

Why This Book Exists

Baseball Money 101 exists because baseball teaches patience better than almost any sport.

It teaches you to respect the process.

To handle failure.

To trust repetition.

To play the long season without panic.

Those same traits determine financial success.

Pat wrote this book for current and former baseball players who understand grind, slumps, adjustments, and the value of fundamentals, but who may never have been taught how money actually works once the game ends.

This is not about becoming rich quickly.

It is about staying steady.

Staying disciplined.

Staying in the game.

Staying Connected

Pat is easy to find through a Google search, on LinkedIn, or on Twitter, where he regularly shares insights on athletes, money, NIL, and life after sports.

If you would like to connect with Pat specifically about *Baseball Money 101,* you can reach him directly at:

info@baseballmoney101.com

Final Thought

Pat's work is rooted in a belief shaped by both football and finance.

Athletes deserve a better playbook for life after sports.

Financial education should arrive before opportunity turns into regret.

The season is long.

Preparation matters.

And fundamentals win in the end.

Part I: Spring Training and Fundamentals

Championships are built on repetition, patience, and fundamentals.

Spring training is where seasons are actually won.

The standings do not matter yet. The crowd is smaller. The games feel slower. But every veteran knows the truth. What happens in spring training determines who is ready when the games start to count. Fundamentals are sharpened. Bad habits are exposed. Reps are stacked day after day, not for attention, but for preparation.

Money works the same way.

Most people want to skip spring training. They want results without reps. They want growth without patience. They want to swing for home runs before they can consistently make contact. Athletes know better. You cannot fake preparation. You cannot cram fundamentals. And you cannot shortcut consistency without paying for it later.

Spring training in baseball is not about proving how good you are. It is about getting back to basics. Footwork. Timing. Mechanics. Situational awareness. Coaches slow the game down so players can speed up later. The goal is not flash. The goal is readiness.

Financial fundamentals serve the same purpose.

This section of the book is not about advanced strategies or complex tactics. It is about building a base that can handle pressure. Cash flow. Saving. Budgeting. Credit awareness. Banking systems. These topics may not feel exciting, but they are what allow everything else to work. Just like baseball, the most important skills are often the least glamorous.

Repetition matters.

In spring training, you take ground balls you have fielded a thousand times. You work counts you already understand. You repeat drills you could do in your sleep. Not because you do not know them, but because consistency erodes without maintenance. Money habits are no different. One good month does not build stability. Repeated behavior does.

Patience matters.

Baseball teaches you that failure is part of the process. You can do everything right and still make an out. You can stay disciplined and still go through a slump. The players who survive are the ones who trust the process and keep showing up. Financial progress works the same way. You will not see immediate results. Accounts grow slowly. Habits take time. That does not mean the system is broken. It means it is working.

Fundamentals matter.

You cannot build a winning season on highlight plays alone. You win by making routine plays consistently. Turning double plays. Hitting cutoff men. Running the bases correctly. Financial fundamentals serve that same role. They prevent small mistakes from becoming big problems. They keep you from playing from behind.

This part of the book is about learning how to play clean baseball with your money.

It is about setting up systems that do not rely on motivation. It is about understanding where your money goes before you decide where you want it to go. It is about protecting yourself so one mistake does not end your season.

Spring training is where you earn the right to compete.

Master the fundamentals here, and everything that comes later becomes easier. Skip them, and no amount of talent or opportunity will save you.

Championships are not built in the spotlight.

They are built in the reps no one sees.

Chapter 1: Why Money Feels Confusing After the Game

Every baseball player remembers the first time the game truly sped up.

The pitcher was quicker than expected. The ball had late movement. The crowd was louder. The margin for error felt thinner. Things you had done a thousand times in practice suddenly felt different under real pressure. It was not because you were unprepared. It was because experience changes how information shows up.

Money works the same way.

Most athletes do not struggle with money because they are careless, reckless, or irresponsible. They struggle because they move from a highly structured environment into one where they are expected to make complex financial decisions without reps, without coaching, and without a system.

One day, baseball sets your schedule.

Practice times. Lifts. Travel. Meals. Meetings.

The next day, the season ends and you are expected to manage income, expenses, credit, taxes, and long-term decisions on your own.

No walkthroughs.

No film sessions.

No playbook.

That is why money feels confusing after the game.

Why Financial Literacy Is Rarely Taught to Athletes

Athletes grow up in systems designed to remove distractions.

Coaches handle logistics so players can focus on performance. Schools manage eligibility. Programs manage travel, meals, and structure. That environment is intentional. It works.

The problem shows up when that structure disappears.

Financial education is often treated as someone else's responsibility. Schools assume families will teach it. Families assume athletes will learn later. Programs focus on winning games, not preparing players for paychecks.

By the time money shows up, the education is already late.

Baseball teaches you how to study pitchers, read scouting reports, and make in-game adjustments. It rarely teaches you how to read a bank statement, understand a credit score, or plan for taxes.

That gap is not a failure of intelligence. It is a failure of timing.

Athletes are expected to figure money out on the fly, the same way a rookie would be expected to hit without batting practice. The confusion is predictable.

Money Myths Passed Through Clubhouses

Every clubhouse has financial advice.

Someone knows a guy who made a fortune flipping real estate. Someone swears the stock market is gambling. Someone else claims saving is pointless if you are not investing aggressively. The loudest voice often sounds the most confident, and confidence spreads fast.

Common myths sound like this:

"If you are not investing, you are falling behind."

"You have to be aggressive to win."

"Saving is for people who do not make enough."

"Debt is either always bad or basically free money."

These ideas spread because they are simple. They are emotional. And they feel actionable.

They are also incomplete or flat-out wrong.

Baseball does not operate on myths. You would never change your swing because someone said it worked for them once. You would not abandon fundamentals because a teammate hit a lucky home run. Money deserves the same discipline.

Clubhouse talk is not a strategy. It is noise.

Saving vs Investing vs Gambling

This confusion causes more damage than almost anything else.

Saving, investing, and gambling are not the same thing. Treating them as interchangeable is like confusing batting practice, a game plan, and backyard home run derbies.

Saving is about protection.

Savings give you stability. Emergency funds. Short-term needs. Margin for error. Savings are liquid, accessible, and boring by design.

In baseball terms, saving is conditioning. It keeps you on the field. You do not win games because of conditioning, but you lose games without it.

Investing is about ownership and growth.

Investing means owning productive assets over time. Businesses. Markets. Long-term systems. It requires patience and discipline. Ups and downs are normal. Results come from staying in the system.

In baseball terms, investing is running the offense over a full season. You trust the process. You accept slumps. You keep showing up.

Gambling is chasing outcomes without a plan.

No protection. No margin. Emotion-driven decisions. Short-term thinking. Gambling feels exciting because it promises immediate results.

In baseball terms, gambling is swinging for the fences every pitch, regardless of count, situation, or defense. Sometimes it works. Most of the time, it does not.

Many athletes skip saving because it feels slow. They jump straight into investing or speculation. That is like skipping spring training and expecting to play 162 games without consequences.

Why Consistency Beats Home-Run Swings

Baseball is a game of repetition.

The same swing.

The same footwork.

The same approach.

Highlights are memorable. They are not what keeps players in the lineup.

Money works the same way.

You do not need the perfect budget. You need a simple one you can run consistently.

You do not need the perfect investment strategy. You need discipline over time.

You do not need to know everything. You need to start and keep showing up.

Consistency builds confidence. Confidence builds discipline. Discipline builds results.

Athletes who succeed financially are not chasing big wins. They are stacking good at-bats. They are avoiding strikeouts caused by impatience. They are staying in position.

Home-run swings look good on social media. Singles win seasons.

Coach's Perspective

If a coach were talking about money, the message would sound familiar.

Do your job.

Make the simple play.

Control what you can control.

We do not take plays off.

Trust the process.

Money does not need heroics. It needs fundamentals. Fundamentals hold up under pressure. That is why great coaches never stop teaching them.

Game Situations and Decision Points

You get your first real paycheck.

Do you spend first and hope there is something left, or protect part of it immediately?

You hear about a hot investment.

Do you chase it without understanding, or stick to a plan you can execute?

You realize you have no emergency savings.

Do you ignore it and hope nothing happens, or start building protection now?

Just like baseball, the decision matters more than the moment.

Common Athlete Mistakes and Financial Parallels

Athletes get impatient.

Financially, that shows up as chasing quick wins.

Athletes trust confidence over preparation.

Financially, that shows up as following bad advice.

Athletes hate feeling behind.

Financially, that leads to forcing decisions.

The same mistakes that lose games lose money.

Winning the Long Game

Baseball careers are short. Financial lives are long.

You do not need to win today. You need to stay in the game. Progress beats perfection. The players who succeed long after the final out are the ones who treat money like a season, not a single at-bat.

This chapter is not about making you rich quickly.

It is about helping you stop feeling lost, rushed, or pressured. It is about building a foundation that allows everything else to work.

Athlete Takeaways

- Spring training matters. Fundamentals come before flash.
- Saving protects you. Investing grows you. Gambling guesses.
- Clubhouse money talk is not a game plan.
- Consistency beats home-run swings.
- Stack good at-bats and stay disciplined.

Chapter 2: Read the Box Score: Your Financial Snapshot

Every baseball player learns this early.

You might remember one great swing, one bad call, or one mistake that sticks with you, but the box score tells the real story. At-bats. Hits. Walks. Strikeouts. Errors. Runs allowed. It does not care how confident you felt or how close the play was. It shows what actually happened.

Money has a box score too.

Most former athletes avoid it. Not because they are irresponsible, but because no one ever taught them how to read it. Bank balances feel scattered. Bills hit at different times. Spending happens automatically. Instead of checking the numbers, people rely on gut feel.

That is how small problems quietly turn into big ones.

Before you change anything, you need to know the score.

Income, Expenses, and Cash Flow

Cash flow is how money moves through your life.

Income is what comes in.

Paychecks. Bonuses. Side work. NIL income for some athletes.

Expenses are what go out.

Rent. Food. Transportation. Insurance. Subscriptions. Lifestyle spending.

Cash flow is the difference between the two.

In baseball terms, income is runs scored. Expenses are runs allowed. Cash flow tells you whether you are winning or digging yourself into a hole.

A lot of athletes focus only on income. More money feels like progress. But if spending rises just as fast, nothing actually improves. That is like scoring four runs but giving up five every game. You might feel productive, but the standings do not lie.

Positive cash flow gives you options.

Negative cash flow puts you under pressure.

You do not need complicated spreadsheets to understand this. You need awareness.

Know what comes in.

Know what goes out.

Everything else builds from there.

Assets, Liabilities, and Net Worth

This is where many athletes get tripped up.

Assets are things you own that have value.

Cash. Investments. Property. Businesses.

Liabilities are what you owe.

Credit cards. Student loans. Car loans. Mortgages.

Net worth is the difference between the two.

In baseball terms, assets are your strengths. Liabilities are vulnerabilities. Net worth is the overall matchup.

One strong asset does not erase multiple weaknesses. Just like one great hitter does not fix a lineup full of holes. You have to look at the whole roster.

Many athletes confuse income with wealth.

Income is what you earn.

Net worth is what you keep and build over time.

A player can sign a contract and still be losing the financial game if liabilities are growing faster than assets. The box score does not care how impressive the deal looked. It only reflects the outcome.

Fixed vs Variable Expenses

Not all expenses are created equal.

Fixed expenses stay mostly consistent.

Rent or mortgage. Insurance. Loan payments. Phone plans.

Variable expenses change month to month.

Food. Travel. Entertainment. Convenience spending.

In baseball terms, fixed expenses are your starting rotation. They define structure. Variable expenses are bullpen decisions. That is where games are often won or lost.

Most people try to cut big fixed costs first, which is often difficult. You cannot easily move mid-season. You cannot instantly change insurance or loan terms.

The real leverage is usually in variable spending you barely notice.

Takeout meals.

Subscription creep.

Impulse purchases.

"Just this once" spending that repeats.

These are unearned runs. One at a time, they do not feel dangerous. Over a season, they change the outcome.

Small leaks sink long seasons.

Film Study on Where Your Money Actually Goes

This is the most uncomfortable part of the process.

It is also the most important.

Pull your bank and credit card statements. Look at them honestly. No judgment. No excuses. Just facts.

Film study is not punishment. It is improvement.

You are not watching tape to feel bad. You are watching tape to get better.

You might notice:

Subscriptions you forgot existed

Convenience spending that adds up faster than expected

Habits that do not match what you say matters to you

If you never look at the film, you keep repeating the same mistakes. Avoiding statements does not protect you. It just delays awareness.

The numbers are not there to shame you. They are there to help you adjust.

Every great team studies film. Even after wins.

Especially after wins.

Why Avoiding the Box Score Creates Stress

Many athletes avoid their financial snapshot because they are afraid of what they will see.

That fear is understandable.

But uncertainty creates more stress than clarity. When you do not know the score, every decision feels heavier. Every expense feels risky. Every opportunity feels confusing.

Once you know the numbers, the pressure eases.

You may not love what you see, but now you have control. Control leads to confidence. Confidence leads to better decisions.

This is how you stop playing from behind.

Coach's Perspective

A coach would never let a team guess how they performed.

The film does not lie.

The box score does not lie.

Details matter.

If you do not look at it, you cannot fix it.

Avoiding the numbers does not change them. Reviewing them gives you power.

That is accountability.

Game Situations and Decision Points

You feel like you are doing fine, but your account balance never grows.

Do you blame income, or review spending?

You get a raise.

Do you upgrade your lifestyle immediately, or improve cash flow first?

You have debt but no clear picture of what you owe.

Do you ignore it, or list it out and face it?

Just like baseball, progress starts with honest evaluation.

Common Athlete Mistakes and Financial Parallels

Athletes rely on feel instead of film.

Financially, that means guessing instead of tracking.

Athletes avoid bad tape.

Financially, that means avoiding statements.

Athletes overvalue one good game.

Financially, that means one big paycheck hiding poor habits.

The scoreboard always catches up.

Winning the Long Game

Great teams know the score at all times, not just at the end of the game. Knowing your financial snapshot is not about judgment. It is about awareness.

Awareness leads to control.

Control leads to confidence.

Confidence leads to discipline.

This chapter is not asking you to be perfect.

It is asking you to be honest.

Once you know the score, every other chapter in this book becomes easier to execute.

Athlete Takeaways

- Read the box score before you change the game plan
- Income means nothing without positive cash flow
- Assets build strength. Liabilities create pressure
- Fixed expenses create structure. Variable expenses decide outcomes
- Watch the film. Awareness puts you back in control

Chapter 3: Playing Small Ball: Budgeting and Saving

Every baseball coach believes in small ball.

Move the runner. Take the extra base. Put the ball in play. Do the little things right over and over again. It is not flashy. It does not make highlight reels. But over a long season, small ball wins games.

Money works the same way.

Most financial struggles are not caused by one massive mistake. They are caused by a thousand small decisions made without a system. Spending here. Skipping savings there. Hoping it works out in the end. That is not a game plan. That is swinging for the fences every at-bat and wondering why the season falls apart.

Budgeting and saving are small ball.

They are not exciting. They are not dramatic. But they put you in position to win consistently.

Why Athletes Resist Budgeting

Many athletes hear the word "budget" and immediately shut down.

It sounds restrictive.

It sounds boring.

It sounds like someone telling you what you cannot do.

That reaction makes sense. You spent years being coached, scheduled, and controlled. When sports end, freedom feels earned. Budgeting can feel like losing that freedom.

But a budget is not punishment.

It is structure.

In baseball terms, budgeting is knowing the situation before you step into the box. Runners on base. Outs. Count. Score. You are not guessing. You are informed.

Without a budget, every spending decision is reactive. You spend based on mood, stress, or convenience. That is like swinging at every pitch and hoping talent carries you.

Talent alone does not win long seasons.

Budgeting Systems That Actually Work

A budget does not need to be complicated to be effective.

The best budgeting systems share a few traits:

They are simple

They are realistic

They are repeatable

If your system requires daily tracking, complex categories, or constant adjustments, you will not stick with it. Coaches do not install plays players cannot execute under pressure. Your budget should work the same way.

At its core, budgeting answers three questions:

How much comes in?

What has to go out?

What is left to deploy intentionally?

That is the offense.

Some people like percentage-based systems.

Some like category-based systems.

Some like separating money into different accounts.

The specific method matters less than consistency.

A budget is successful if you actually use it.

You are not trying to control every dollar. You are trying to control direction. Small adjustments over time create massive results.

Playing Small Ball With Your Money

Small ball is about steady progress.

Singles. Walks. Sacrifice bunts.

They do not look impressive alone.

They add up fast.

Saving works the same way.

Many athletes think saving only matters when income is high. That is backwards. Saving is a habit before it is a number.

You do not need to save a lot to start.

You need to save consistently.

In baseball terms, saving is getting on base. You cannot score if you never reach first.

Skipping savings because it feels insignificant is like refusing to take a walk because it does not look cool. Over a season, those walks change outcomes.

Automating Savings Like Daily Reps

No player debates whether to take reps.

You hit off the tee.

You take ground balls.

You throw bullpen sessions.

You do not wait to see if you feel motivated. Reps are built into the schedule.

Saving should work the same way.

If you wait to save what is left over, you will almost never save anything. Life fills the space. Spending expands. Convenience wins.

Automation fixes that.

Direct deposit into savings

Automatic transfers on payday

Scheduled contributions to investment accounts

In baseball terms, automation is your daily work. It happens whether you are tired or energized. The reps compound.

You are not relying on willpower. You are building a system.

Systems beat motivation every time.

Emergency Funds as Injury Insurance

Every athlete understands injury risk.

You do not plan to get hurt.

You prepare anyway.

Training staff. Rehab plans. Depth charts. Recovery protocols.

An emergency fund is the financial version of that preparation.

It is cash set aside for the unexpected:

Car repairs

Medical bills

Job changes

Delayed income

Family emergencies

Without an emergency fund, every surprise becomes a crisis. You reach for credit. You panic. You abandon your plan.

With an emergency fund, you stay composed. You handle the situation and keep playing.

That is staying in the game.

Emergency funds are not about return. They are about control. They give you time and options when pressure hits.

Most athletes underestimate how powerful that is.

How Much Is Enough

There is no magic number.

A common target is three to six months of essential expenses. That is not a finish line. It is a guideline.

Early in your career, even one month is a win. Progress matters more than perfection.

In baseball terms, this is depth. You hope you never need it. When you do, it saves the season.

Build it slowly. Protect it. Do not treat it like spending money.

Balancing Lifestyle With Long-Term Wins

This is where many former athletes struggle the most.

You worked hard.

You sacrificed.

You feel like you deserve to enjoy life.

That feeling is valid.

The mistake is letting short-term rewards quietly destroy long-term flexibility.

Lifestyle creep happens when spending rises automatically with income. Better car. Better apartment. More convenience. None of it feels reckless. Over time, it creates pressure.

Baseball teaches delayed gratification.

You take extra reps when nobody is watching so you can perform when it matters. Money requires the same discipline.

You do not have to live like a minor leaguer forever. You do have to be intentional.

Spend on what matters.

Cut what does not.

Protect future options.

Lifestyle should support your life, not limit it.

Why Small Ball Beats Home Runs

Everyone loves the home run.

Big investment wins.

Sudden income jumps.

Perfect timing.

They are rare.

What is repeatable is small ball.

Saving every paycheck

Staying under budget

Avoiding unnecessary debt

Building reserves

These decisions do not feel dramatic. Over a decade, they separate winners from regret.

Most financial success stories look boring up close. They are built on discipline, not luck.

Coach's Perspective

A coach would not overcomplicate this.

Do your job.

Be consistent.

Trust the system.

Do not cheat the work.

Budgets and savings are boring for the same reason practice drills are boring.

They work.

Game Situations and Decision Points

You get paid.

Do you save first or hope there is something left?

You want to upgrade your lifestyle.

Do you check the plan or ignore it?

An unexpected expense hits.

Do you stay calm or reach for credit?

These are inning-by-inning decisions. Over time, they decide seasons.

Common Athlete Mistakes and Financial Parallels

Athletes skip fundamentals.

Financially, that looks like skipping savings.

Athletes overestimate what they can handle.

Financially, that leads to no emergency fund.

Athletes reward effort with shortcuts.

Financially, that shows up as lifestyle creep.

The same habits that lose games lose money.

Winning the Long Game

Small ball does not win headlines. It wins seasons.

Budgeting and saving give you control. Control creates freedom. Freedom allows you to make decisions from strength, not stress.

This is how you stay composed when pressure shows up.

You are not trying to hit a financial home run every year. You are trying to stay in the lineup for decades.

Athlete Takeaways

- Run a simple offense you can execute every month
- Save first and make it automatic. Reps matter
- Emergency funds keep you calm when pressure hits
- Lifestyle choices today affect flexibility tomorrow
- Small ball wins long seasons

Chapter 4: Credit, Debt, and Playing With the Count

Every baseball player understands the count.

Ball and strike awareness changes everything. When you are ahead in the count, you can be selective. You can look for your pitch. You can let mistakes come to you. When you fall behind, the game speeds up. You protect the plate. You expand the zone. One bad swing can end the at-bat.

Credit and debt work the same way.

Borrowed money puts you in a count. Used well, it gives you flexibility and leverage. Used poorly, it forces defensive decisions and limits your options. Most financial trouble does not come from one catastrophic swing. It comes from slowly falling behind in the count and never getting back to even.

Understanding credit and debt is not about fear. It is about situational awareness.

How Credit Scores and Reports Actually Work

Your credit score is not a judgment of who you are.

It is a scoreboard.

It measures how you have handled borrowed money over time. Nothing more. Nothing less.

Credit scoring looks at a few core factors:

Do you pay on time?

How much of your available credit do you use?

How long have you been using credit?

How often do you apply for new credit?

In baseball terms, credit is trust from the coaching staff.

If you show up on time, execute the fundamentals, and do not make the same mistake twice, trust grows. If you miss assignments or make careless errors, trust disappears quickly.

Your credit report is the film.

Your credit score is the grade.

You cannot argue with film. You can only improve how you play next time.

That is important for athletes to understand. Credit improves through behavior, not shortcuts. There is no trick swing that fixes it overnight.

Why Credit Matters Even If You Hate Debt

Some athletes want nothing to do with credit.

They have seen teammates get buried by it. They associate debt with stress, mistakes, and regret. That reaction makes sense.

But ignoring credit does not eliminate it. It limits options.

Credit affects:

Housing approval

Interest rates

Insurance pricing

Business opportunities

Flexibility during transitions

In baseball terms, refusing to understand the count does not stop the pitcher from throwing strikes. It just makes you reactive instead of prepared.

You do not have to love credit. You do have to understand it.

Credit Cards, Loans, and Interest

Credit cards and loans are tools.

Like any tool, they can help or hurt depending on how you use them.

Interest is the cost of borrowing. It is the opposing team scoring runs every inning you leave runners on base. The longer balances sit, the more expensive they become.

Carrying high-interest balances is like playing extra innings every night. You can still compete, but fatigue builds. Mistakes compound. Momentum shifts against you.

Used correctly, credit cards can:

Smooth cash flow

Provide short-term flexibility

Build credit history

Used poorly, they become:

Lifestyle enablers

Stress multipliers

Long-term anchors

Loans work the same way. Mortgages, student loans, and business loans can be strategic. Consumer debt for convenience and status rarely is.

Borrowed money should be intentional, not automatic.

Playing Ahead vs Playing Behind in the Count

When you are ahead in the count, you dictate the at-bat.

You wait for a pitch you can drive. You do not chase. You stay disciplined.

Financially, that looks like:

Low balances

Strong payment history

Adequate savings

Flexibility if income changes

When you are behind in the count, everything changes.

You protect instead of attack. You take what you can get. You worry more about survival than strategy.

Financially, that looks like:

High balances

Minimum payments

No emergency fund

Stress-driven decisions

Debt is not inherently bad. Being permanently behind in the count is.

Good Debt vs Bad Debt

Not all debt is the same.

Good debt helps you build something that creates future options.

Education that increases earning potential

A reasonably priced home

A business investment with a plan

Bad debt finances consumption.

Lifestyle upgrades

Status purchases

Impulse spending

Short-term pleasure with long-term payments

In baseball terms, good debt is investing in development. Extra coaching. Better training. Equipment that improves performance. Bad debt is swinging for the fences every pitch and hoping it works out.

The difference is not the interest rate alone. It is whether the debt helps you advance runners or leaves you stranded.

Ask one simple question before taking on debt:

Does this create future flexibility, or does it reduce it?

The Most Common Debt Traps for Athletes

Debt problems usually start quietly.

Using credit to fund lifestyle

Ignoring balances because payments feel manageable

Co-signing without understanding the risk

Assuming future income will fix today's decisions

Athletes are especially vulnerable to these traps.

You are trained to believe effort solves problems. On the field, that is often true. Financially, effort does not erase math.

Debt does not care how hard you work. It only cares how consistently you pay.

Co-signing is one of the most dangerous traps. It feels like loyalty. It feels like helping a teammate. In reality, it is taking responsibility for someone else's mistakes.

In baseball terms, it is covering a position you were never assigned and getting burned when the play breaks down.

How Small Debt Mistakes End Seasons Early

One missed payment does not ruin a career.

A pattern does.

Late payments compound.

Balances creep higher.

Interest eats progress.

Stress affects decisions.

Suddenly, options disappear. Housing choices shrink. Job flexibility drops. Everything feels tighter.

That is how seasons end early. Not with one dramatic strikeout, but with a slow erosion of fundamentals.

How to Reset the Count

If you are already behind, the goal is not heroics.

It is getting back to even.

List out every debt.

Understand interest rates.

Stop adding new balances.

Create a payoff plan you can actually execute.

This is small ball again. Singles. Walks. Productive outs.

Trying to fix debt overnight usually backfires. Discipline over time wins.

Coach's Perspective

A coach would be blunt.

Know the count.

Do not chase bad pitches.

Protect the zone.

Value every at-bat.

Debt magnifies mistakes. Discipline keeps you in control.

You do not need to be perfect. You do need to be consistent.

Game Situations and Decision Points

You can put it on a card.

Is it part of the plan or just convenient?

You qualify for a loan.

Do you ask if you should take it or just if you can?

Someone asks you to co-sign.

Do you understand the downside, or are you reacting emotionally?

These are late-inning decisions. Awareness matters.

Common Athlete Mistakes and Financial Parallels

Athletes chase comfort early.

Financially, that becomes lifestyle debt.

Athletes trust momentum too much.

Financially, that leads to over-borrowing.

Athletes ignore small mistakes.

Financially, that becomes long-term damage.

The game punishes repeated mental errors.

Winning the Long Game

Debt can be a tool or a trap.

Used intentionally, it supports growth. Used emotionally, it limits your future. The goal is not to avoid credit entirely. The goal is to stay ahead in the count.

Play disciplined at-bats. Protect flexibility. Let opportunities come to you instead of forcing swings.

That is how long careers are built.

Athlete Takeaways

- Credit is trust. Protect it like your spot in the lineup
- Interest works against you when you lose discipline
- Borrow to build, not to impress
- Know the count before you swing
- Staying ahead in the count keeps you in the game

Chapter 5: The Dugout of Money: Banking Basics

Every baseball team has a dugout.

It is not where the highlights happen. Nobody buys tickets to watch players sit on the bench. But every coach knows this: if the dugout is disorganized, distracted, or sloppy, the game eventually unravels. Bats go missing. Signs get missed. Players lose focus. Small problems turn into momentum killers.

Your banking system is the dugout of your money.

It is where everything starts and where everything resets between plays. Paychecks come in. Bills go out. Decisions pause there before the next move. When your banking setup is clean and intentional, money flows smoothly. When it is chaotic, even strong income and good intentions break down.

Before you think about investing, growth, or long-term strategy, your dugout has to function.

Why Banking Feels Boring but Decides Everything

Most athletes do not think much about banking.

You open an account when someone tells you to. You swipe a card. You move on. As long as nothing breaks, it feels fine.

That mindset works until it does not.

Fees start showing up. Payments miss. Fraud hits. Transfers bounce. Suddenly you are reacting instead of executing. Stress increases, and money decisions start happening under pressure.

In baseball terms, this is ignoring the dugout until the lineup card is wrong and no one knows who is hitting next.

Banking is not exciting. It is foundational. The teams that win long seasons are the ones that handle the basics cleanly every day.

Checking vs Savings Accounts

Checking and savings accounts serve different roles. Mixing them usually creates confusion.

Checking accounts are for movement.

This is where money flows in and out. Paychecks, bill payments, debit card spending, subscriptions, and everyday transactions all live here.

Savings accounts are for storage.

This is money with purpose. Emergency funds. Short-term goals. Buffers. Protection.

In baseball terms, checking is the field. Savings is the dugout.

If all your money is on the field all the time, you are exposed. One bad hop, one unexpected play, and you are scrambling. If all your money sits in the dugout, nothing is happening. You are safe, but you are not advancing.

The mistake most people make is using one account for everything. That is like playing an entire season without separating offense and defense. It works until pressure hits.

Separation creates clarity.

When savings is not easily touched, you think before spending it. When checking is designed for flow, you can manage timing without panic.

Why Every Player Needs a Buffer

Checking accounts should not be run at zero.

A small buffer prevents overdrafts, fees, and stress when timing does not line up perfectly. Deposits get delayed. Payments process early. Mistakes happen.

In baseball terms, this is having a runner on first instead of bases empty. You have margin. You are not one miscue away from trouble.

Savings accounts provide deeper protection. Emergency funds exist so unexpected events do not force you into debt or desperation. Car repairs. Medical bills. Job changes. Travel emergencies. Life happens.

Strong teams expect randomness. Strong financial systems do too.

Online Banks vs Traditional Banks

There is no single right answer here.

Traditional banks offer physical branches, tellers, and face-to-face service. Online banks often offer lower fees, better interest rates, and easier automation.

The right choice is the one that fits your system.

Some athletes value walking into a branch. Others value efficiency and low cost. What matters is understanding how your bank works, what it charges, and how accessible your money is when you need it.

In baseball terms, this is roster construction. Some teams value veterans. Some value youth. Both can win if the system fits the personnel.

Ask yourself:

How easy is it to move money?

What fees am I paying?

How quickly can I access cash?

How reliable is customer support?

Do not choose a bank because someone else likes it. Choose one that fits how you actually live.

How Money Moves Electronically

Money does not move instantly, even if it feels that way.

Behind the scenes, banking relies on systems with rules, delays, and cut-off times. Direct deposit, ACH transfers, debit transactions, and automatic payments all follow different timelines.

Understanding this matters.

Overdrafts usually happen because of timing, not irresponsibility. A payment clears before a deposit posts. A transfer takes longer than expected. A weekend delays processing.

In baseball terms, this is knowing the game clock and substitution rules. If you do not understand timing, you end up with the wrong player in the wrong spot.

Know when:

Paychecks hit

Bills process

Transfers clear

Automatic payments draft

That awareness prevents unnecessary mistakes.

Automation as Dugout Discipline

Good teams eliminate avoidable errors.

Automation helps do that financially.

Direct deposit for income

Automatic bill pay for fixed expenses

Scheduled transfers to savings

Automation removes decision fatigue. You are not relying on memory, motivation, or willpower. Systems run whether you feel disciplined or not.

In baseball terms, this is having signs nailed down so everyone knows what is happening without confusion.

Automation does not mean ignoring accounts. It means reducing the number of things that can go wrong.

Protecting Yourself From Fraud

Fraud is not rare. It is part of the environment.

Cards get skimmed. Accounts get hacked. Information gets exposed. The question is not whether fraud exists. It is how quickly you catch it.

Protection comes from habits, not paranoia.

Check accounts regularly

Set alerts for transactions and balances

Use strong passwords and two-factor authentication

Separate savings from daily spending

In baseball terms, this is defensive positioning. You are not guessing where the ball will go. You are ready when it does.

Most fraud damage happens because people do not look. A clean system makes problems obvious early, when they are easiest to fix.

Overdrafts and Fees: The Unforced Errors

Overdraft fees and bank charges are the financial version of throwing errors.

They do not come from lack of talent. They come from lack of attention.

Running accounts too tight

Not understanding timing

Using one account for everything

Ignoring alerts

Each fee may seem small. Over a season, they add up and drain momentum.

Great teams eliminate unforced errors. Clean banking does the same.

Coach's Perspective

A coach would not sugarcoat this.

Protect the dugout.

Details matter.

Handle your business.

Do not create your own problems.

Banking is not about brilliance. It is about discipline. The basics executed well keep you composed when the game gets tight.

Game Situations and Decision Points

You have one account for everything.

Do you separate systems or keep guessing?

You get hit with a fee.

Do you adjust the system or ignore it?

You notice a charge you do not recognize.

Do you act immediately or hope it resolves itself?

These moments feel small. Over time, they define outcomes.

Common Athlete Mistakes and Financial Parallels

Athletes ignore details.

Financially, that shows up as fees and errors.

Athletes trust systems blindly.

Financially, that leads to missed fraud or mistakes.

Athletes avoid boring work.

Financially, that creates chaos later.

The game punishes lack of attention.

Winning the Long Game

A clean dugout supports everything else.

Good banking does not make headlines. It does not feel impressive. But it keeps you organized, protected, and ready to execute when opportunity shows up.

You cannot run an offense without knowing who is up next. You cannot build wealth without knowing where your money lives and how it moves.

Handle the dugout, and the rest of the game slows down.

Athlete Takeaways

- Checking is for movement, savings is for protection
- Separate accounts create clarity and control
- Know how and when your money moves
- Automation reduces unforced errors
- A clean dugout keeps you ready to win

Part II: Defense and Protection

You cannot win without protecting what you earn.

Every baseball player understands this truth early.

You can have a great swing, a hot bat, and a deep lineup, but if you cannot play defense, the game slips away fast. Errors extend innings. Missed cutoffs turn singles into doubles. A dropped fly ball changes momentum. Defense rarely shows up in highlight reels, but it decides seasons.

Money works the same way.

You can earn well. You can invest aggressively. You can chase growth and opportunity. But without protection, one mistake, one injury, one lawsuit, or one poorly timed event can undo years of progress. Defense is what keeps you in the game long enough for offense to matter.

This part of the book is about defense.

Not fear-based defense. Not playing scared. Smart, disciplined protection that allows you to stay aggressive when it actually makes sense.

Why Athletes Struggle With Financial Defense

Athletes are trained to focus on performance.

Score more runs. Hit for power. Throw harder. Move faster. That mindset builds offense. It does not automatically build protection.

In sports, coaches design the defense. Positioning, backups, coverage schemes, and contingency plans are handled for you. In life, that responsibility shifts entirely to you.

No one sets your coverage.

No one checks your blind spots.

No one calls time-out when risk creeps in.

So most athletes focus on earning and spending and ignore protection until something breaks.

That is not a flaw. It is a gap in coaching.

Defense Is About Availability

In baseball, availability matters.

It does not matter how talented you are if an injury sidelines you. It does not matter how good your bat is if one bad play costs the team the game.

Financially, availability works the same way.

If one unexpected event forces you into debt, drains your savings, or derails your long-term plan, you were not protected. Defense is what keeps you available to keep playing the long season.

Insurance.

Cash reserves.

Risk awareness.

Liability protection.

These are not luxuries. They are how you stay on the field.

The Goal of Protection Is Not Perfection

Great defenders do not try to eliminate all risk.

They position well.

They anticipate.

They reduce the damage when things go wrong.

You cannot prevent every bad hop. You cannot predict every injury. You cannot eliminate every financial risk.

But you can limit exposure.

You can make sure one mistake does not turn into a disaster. You can make sure one bad inning does not end the season.

That is the role of defense.

Offense Plays Better With Good Defense

Here is what most people miss.

Strong defense actually allows better offense.

When you know you are protected, you can swing freely. You can invest with patience. You can make long-term decisions without panic. You are not forcing plays because you are afraid of what happens if something goes wrong.

Teams with weak defense play tight. They press. They rush. They force offense because they know one mistake could end everything.

Financially, the same thing happens.

Lack of protection leads to emotional decisions.

Strong protection leads to discipline.

What This Section Will Teach You

Part II focuses on the defensive side of your financial game.

You will learn how to think about risk realistically, not emotionally. You will learn how insurance actually works and what coverage matters at different stages of life. You will learn how to protect income, assets, and future opportunities without overcomplicating things.

This is not about buying everything.

This is not about playing scared.

This is about playing smart.

Defense is how you stay in the game long enough to win it.

The Long Season Mindset

Baseball seasons are long.

Slumps happen.

Injuries happen.

Bad calls happen.

Unexpected breaks happen.

Teams that survive understand one thing: you cannot control everything, but you can prepare for most things.

Money is no different.

You do not win financially by avoiding risk altogether. You win by protecting what you earn so time, consistency, and discipline can do their work.

That is defense.

And defense is how championships are actually won.

Chapter 6: Risk Awareness and Smart Decision Making

Knowing When to Swing and When to Take a Pitch

Every baseball player knows this moment.

You step into the box. The count is full. The pitcher has a good arm, maybe a nasty breaking ball. The crowd is loud. Your instincts say swing. Your ego wants to make something happen. But the best hitters pause for a split second and ask a better question:

What's the situation?

Score. Inning. Count. Pitcher. Your strengths. The on-deck hitter. Risk in baseball is never just about whether you *can* swing. It's about whether you *should*.

Money decisions work the exact same way.

Most financial mistakes are not made because people are lazy or reckless. They are made because risk is misunderstood. Athletes, in particular, are wired to compete, to trust confidence, and to believe they can recover from mistakes. That mindset wins games. Financially, it can create exposure if it is not paired with awareness.

This chapter is about understanding risk the same way great hitters understand the strike zone.

Emotional Risk vs Financial Risk

Emotional risk is how you *feel* about uncertainty.

Financial risk is how much damage you can actually absorb.

Athletes often confuse the two.

You have competed under pressure your whole life. You are comfortable taking big shots. You trust yourself to bounce back after a mistake. Emotionally, that creates a high tolerance for risk.

Financially, the reality may be very different.

If one bad decision would:

- Force you into debt
- Wipe out your savings
- Push you to sell investments at the wrong time
- Limit career or life options

then your financial risk tolerance is lower than your confidence suggests.

In baseball terms, this is the difference between *liking* to hit with two strikes and actually being good at it. Wanting the moment does not mean it fits the situation.

Smart players know when they are the right option and when the team needs something else.

Time Horizon: The Inning Matters

Risk changes depending on timing.

Money you need soon should not be exposed to big swings.

Money you will not touch for decades can handle more volatility.

This is called time horizon, and it is one of the most important concepts in financial decision-making.

In baseball terms:

- Late innings with a one-run lead call for contact and discipline

- Early innings allow more patience and selective aggression

If you are early in your career, building savings, and investing for long-term goals, short-term volatility matters less. If you need money in the next year or two, risk needs to be controlled.

Many athletes make the mistake of swinging the same way in every inning.

Same approach. Same aggression. Same risk.

Baseball punishes that. So does money.

Flexibility Is the Hidden Variable

Two players can face the same pitch and have very different outcomes.

Why?

Because one has support behind them.

Depth matters in baseball. A team with bench depth and a strong bullpen can take more chances. A team stretched thin has to play conservative.

Financial flexibility works the same way.

Flexibility comes from:

- Emergency savings
- Stable income
- Low fixed expenses
- Manageable debt
- Insurance coverage

The more flexibility you have, the more risk you can responsibly take. The less flexibility you have, the more disciplined your decisions must be.

Ignoring flexibility is like ignoring the bullpen when deciding whether to pull the starter. You might get away with it once. Over a season, it costs you games.

How Risk Impacts Every Money Decision

Risk is not just about investing.

It affects:

- How much cash you keep
- How much debt you take on
- What insurance coverage you need
- How aggressive your lifestyle choices are
- How concentrated your investments become

Every financial decision carries downside. Pretending otherwise does not make you bold. It makes you unprepared.

A simple filter helps:

What happens if this does not go my way?

In baseball, players are taught to think two plays ahead. Where's the cutoff? What's the backup? Where's the throw if something goes wrong?

Money requires the same awareness.

Knowing When to Swing and When to Take a Pitch

Great hitters are not aggressive all the time.

They swing at pitches they can handle.

They take pitches that don't fit the count.

They trust the process.

Financially:

- Sometimes the right move is to invest aggressively
- Sometimes the right move is to protect cash
- Sometimes the smartest decision is doing nothing

The mistake is playing one speed all the time.

Always aggressive leads to overexposure.

Always conservative leads to stagnation.

Winning decisions are situational, not emotional.

Coach's Perspective

If a coach were talking about money, the message would sound familiar.

- **"Know the situation."**
- **"Don't put the team in a bad spot."**
- **"Control what you can control."**
- **"Play the count."**
- **"Make the smart play."**

Risk is part of the game. Poor awareness is optional.

Great teams do not avoid risk. They manage it.

Game Situations and Decision Points

Situation 1:

You hear about an aggressive investment opportunity with big upside.

Do you ask if it fits your timeline and flexibility, or just if it sounds exciting?

Situation 2:

You consider a major purchase that increases monthly obligations.

Do you evaluate what happens if income changes, or assume everything stays perfect?

Situation 3:

You feel confident and want to "press" financially.

Do you check the downside first, or swing because momentum feels good?

Same game. Same pressure. Same consequences.

Common Athlete Mistakes and Financial Parallels

Athletes trust confidence over context.

Financially, that leads to overexposure.

Athletes chase momentum.

Financially, that leads to poor timing.

Athletes ignore fatigue and limits.

Financially, that leads to stress, panic, and forced decisions.

The skills that make athletes great must be paired with awareness to work financially.

Winning the Long Game

Risk cannot be eliminated.

Loss can be managed.

The athletes who succeed long-term understand their limits and respect them. They swing hard when the pitch is right. They take pitches when it isn't. They stay disciplined even when the crowd wants fireworks.

That is not fear.

That is professionalism.

Athlete Takeaways

- Play the count. Risk depends on the situation, not your ego
- Confidence does not equal capacity. Know your limits
- Time horizon and flexibility decide how aggressive you can be
- Not swinging is sometimes the smartest play
- Smart risk keeps you in the lineup all season

Chapter 7: Insurance Fundamentals Every Player Needs

Staying in the Lineup When Life Makes Contact

Every baseball player learns this early.

You can do everything right and still get hurt.

You can take perfect swings, stretch properly, follow the training plan, and play within the system, and one bad hop or awkward slide can change everything. Baseball is not a contact sport like football, but contact still happens. Collisions at the plate. Fastballs off the hand. Diving catches gone wrong.

That is why organizations invest heavily in trainers, medical staff, depth charts, and contingency plans. They do not assume injuries will not happen. They assume baseball is a long season and availability matters.

Insurance plays that same role in your financial life.

You do not buy insurance because you expect something bad to happen. You buy it because you understand that life includes bad hops. Unexpected events are not failures. They are part of the game.

Ignoring that reality does not make you tough. It makes you exposed.

Why Insurance Is About Staying in the Lineup

In baseball, talent only matters if you can stay on the field.

A star player on the injured list does not help the team. Potential does not win games if you cannot play through the season.

Financially, availability works the same way.

If one unexpected event:

- Drains your savings
- Forces you into debt
- Pushes you to abandon long-term plans
- Creates years of recovery

then you were underprotected.

Insurance exists to protect availability. It keeps one incident from turning into a career-altering setback. It is not about fear. It is about durability.

Championship teams value durability.

Health Insurance Basics

Health insurance is non-negotiable.

Medical costs are one of the fastest ways athletes lose financial momentum. An injury, illness, or emergency can create bills that follow you for years if you are uninsured or underinsured.

Health insurance helps cover:

- Doctor visits
- Prescriptions
- Emergency care
- Surgeries
- Ongoing treatment and recovery

Athletes often assume they are healthy and therefore safe. That mindset works until it does not.

In baseball terms, skipping health insurance is like playing without a helmet because you have not been hit yet. You might feel fine for a while. When contact comes, the consequences are immediate.

Health insurance is also about access:

- Access to preventative care
- Access to early treatment
- Access to recovery instead of avoidance

Know your plan the same way you know the scouting report.

You should understand:

- What services are covered
- Your deductible
- Your out-of-pocket maximum
- What happens in an emergency

Learning this after something goes wrong is like learning the signs during a game. Preparation matters.

Auto and Renters Insurance

Auto insurance protects more than your car.

It protects you from:

- Liability if someone is injured
- Medical costs
- Lawsuits
- Financial responsibility for accidents

Driving without proper coverage is like throwing to a base without checking the runner. The mistake can be costly even if it feels routine.

Renters insurance is often overlooked, especially by younger athletes.

Renters insurance covers:

- Personal property
- Theft or damage
- Liability if someone is injured in your residence

In baseball terms, auto and renters insurance protect field position. One mistake should not turn into a multi-run inning against you.

These policies are relatively inexpensive compared to the damage they prevent. Ignoring them is not aggressive. It is careless.

Homeowners Insurance

If you own a home, homeowners insurance is essential.

It protects:

- The structure
- Your belongings
- Liability exposure

It also covers events most people do not think about until they happen:

- Fires
- Storm damage
- Water issues
- Accidents on your property
- Legal claims

Owning a home without insurance is like playing the outfield without backup. Everything looks fine until one ball gets past you.

Homeownership adds responsibility. Insurance is how you manage that responsibility without putting your entire financial future at risk.

Deductibles, Premiums, and Coverage Limits

This is where confusion usually starts.

Premiums are what you pay to keep coverage active.

Deductibles are what you pay out of pocket before insurance kicks in.

Coverage limits are the maximum amounts the policy will pay.

Higher deductibles usually mean lower premiums.

Lower deductibles usually mean higher premiums.

There is no free lunch.

The goal is balance.

In baseball terms, this is workload management. Too much strain increases injury risk. Too little preparation increases exposure.

You want:

- Premiums you can consistently afford
- Deductibles you can handle without panic
- Coverage limits that actually protect you in a worst-case scenario

Insurance is not about getting every dollar back. It is about preventing financial catastrophe.

Why Being Underinsured Is More Dangerous Than Overpaying

Many athletes choose the cheapest policy without understanding what it does not cover.

That is dangerous.

Saving a small amount on premiums can cost you massively when something goes wrong. Underinsurance feels smart until it fails under pressure.

In baseball terms, this is cutting corners on equipment or rehab. It works until the season grinds you down.

Adequate protection matters more than minimal cost.

Coach's Perspective

A coach would not debate this.

- **"Protect yourself."**
- **"Stay available."**

- **"Handle your business."**
- **"Don't put the team in a bad spot."**

Insurance is part of preparation. Teams that ignore preparation do not survive long seasons.

Game Situations and Decision Points

Situation 1:

You are healthy and considering skipping health coverage to save money.

Are you prepared for the downside if something unexpected happens?

Situation 2:

You choose the cheapest auto policy available.

Do you understand the liability limits and what happens in a serious accident?

Situation 3:

You rent and assume renters insurance is unnecessary.

What happens if your belongings are stolen or someone is injured in your space?

These are not hypothetical decisions. They are season-shaping choices.

Common Athlete Mistakes and Financial Parallels

Athletes underestimate injury risk.

Financially, that means skipping insurance.

Athletes focus on short-term comfort.

Financially, that leads to undercoverage.

Athletes ignore details.

Financially, that leads to surprises when it matters most.

Baseball punishes teams that ignore fundamentals. Life does too.

Winning the Long Game

Insurance does not win games.

It keeps you in them.

You cannot control every bounce, injury, or accident. You can control how prepared you are when it happens. Strong teams respect defense. Strong financial plans respect protection.

Availability wins championships.

Athlete Takeaways

- Insurance keeps you in the lineup when life makes contact
- Health coverage is non-negotiable
- Auto, renters, and homeowners insurance protect field position
- Premiums and deductibles are trade-offs, not shortcuts
- You cannot win the season from the injured list

Chapter 8: Life, Disability, and Liability Coverage

Chapter 8: Life, Disability, and Liability Coverage

Protecting the Franchise, Not Just This Season

Every baseball organization thinks beyond today's lineup.

They do not just plan for tonight's starter. They think about the rotation. The bullpen. The farm system. Long-term contracts. Injury risk. Future payroll. A franchise that only focuses on the next game eventually collapses.

Your financial life works the same way.

Health, auto, and homeowners insurance protect you from immediate setbacks. Life, disability, and liability coverage protect the franchise. They exist to guard against events that do not just interrupt a season but threaten everything you have built.

These coverages are not about fear. They are about responsibility.

Why This Coverage Is About the Franchise

In baseball, a franchise is more than one player.

It is future earnings. Long-term commitments. People who depend on the organization's stability. When a star player goes down long term, the ripple effects matter. Contracts, families, careers, and livelihoods are all connected.

Financially, life, disability, and liability insurance exist because your income and future earning power are your most valuable assets.

If those disappear unexpectedly, the damage is not temporary. It can last decades.

Protecting the franchise means protecting:

- Your income
- Your family
- Your future options
- The people who rely on you

That is grown-up baseball. That is grown-up money.

Term vs Permanent Life Insurance

Life insurance exists to protect others if you are not there.

It replaces income, pays off debts, and gives families time and flexibility instead of panic. The confusion starts when people do not understand the two main types.

Term Life Insurance

Term life insurance covers you for a specific period of time. Ten years. Twenty years. Thirty years.

If you pass away during that term, the policy pays a benefit. If you outlive the term, coverage ends.

In baseball terms, term insurance is a clean, affordable contract that covers your prime years. It protects your family while you are building income, raising kids, paying off debt, and establishing stability.

Term insurance is:

- Simple

- Affordable
- Focused on protection

For most players and former athletes, term insurance is the foundation.

Permanent Life Insurance

Permanent life insurance lasts your entire life and includes a savings or investment component.

It is more expensive. It is more complex. It can be useful in specific situations, such as estate planning or long-term tax strategies, but it is often oversold.

In baseball terms, permanent insurance is a long, complex contract with multiple clauses. It may make sense for certain franchises in certain situations, but it is not something you sign without fully understanding the details.

Permanent insurance should solve a specific problem, not just sound impressive.

The mistake athletes make is buying complexity before they need it.

Disability Insurance and Income Protection

If life insurance protects others when you die, disability insurance protects you while you are alive.

Your ability to earn income is your most valuable asset. Lose it, and everything else is affected.

Disability insurance replaces a portion of your income if you cannot work due to injury or illness.

In baseball terms, this is protecting against a long-term injury that does not end your career but keeps you off the field. You still have a future, but you need support while you recover.

Athletes understand this intuitively. One injury can change everything. Financially, disability insurance keeps one injury from becoming permanent damage.

Key things to understand:

- Short-term vs long-term disability
- How much income is replaced
- How long benefits last
- What qualifies as a disability

Many people assume this will never happen to them. That assumption is expensive.

Most long-term disabilities are not dramatic injuries. They are illnesses, accidents, or conditions that slowly remove your ability to work. Preparation matters.

Umbrella Liability Coverage

Liability is the risk most people underestimate.

If someone is injured and you are found responsible, the costs can exceed standard insurance limits quickly. Lawsuits do not care how disciplined or well-intentioned you are.

Umbrella insurance provides extra liability coverage beyond your auto and homeowners policies.

In baseball terms, umbrella coverage is the deep outfield fence. Most plays never reach it. When they do, you are glad it is there.

Umbrella policies are relatively inexpensive compared to the protection they offer. They matter more as:

- Income increases
- Assets grow
- Public exposure increases

Athletes, former athletes, and high earners are often bigger targets simply because they appear to have more resources.

Ignoring liability risk does not make you humble. It makes you vulnerable.

Common Insurance Mistakes Players Make

This is where athletes get tripped up.

Mistake 1: Buying Too Little Coverage

Choosing the cheapest option without understanding exposure. Saving small money now creates massive risk later.

Mistake 2: Buying the Wrong Type

Permanent insurance sold when term coverage was needed. Complexity added before fundamentals were solid.

Mistake 3: Ignoring Disability Insurance

Assuming income will always be there. One injury or illness proves otherwise.

Mistake 4: No Liability Protection

Assuming auto and homeowners limits are enough. One lawsuit proves they are not.

Mistake 5: Never Reviewing Policies

Life changes. Income changes. Family changes. Coverage that made sense years ago may no longer fit.

In baseball terms, this is playing the wrong position, with the wrong gear, and never checking the scouting report.

Coach's Perspective

A coach would not sugarcoat this.

- **"Protect the franchise."**
- **"Availability matters."**
- **"Handle your business."**
- **"Do not leave yourself exposed."**
- **"Long seasons require depth."**

Insurance is not optional preparation. It is part of being a professional.

Game Situations and Decision Points

Situation 1:

You start a family. Do you increase life insurance or assume nothing will change?

Situation 2:

Your income grows. Do you protect it with disability coverage or trust it will always be there?

Situation 3:

Your assets increase. Do you add liability protection or assume your base coverage is enough?

Just like baseball, ignoring risk does not eliminate it.

Winning the Long Game

Baseball careers end. Financial lives continue.

Life, disability, and liability insurance exist to make sure one moment does not undo decades of effort. They protect people you care about. They protect future choices. They protect dignity.

Strong franchises think long-term. Strong financial plans do the same.

Athlete Takeaways

- Protect the franchise, not just today's lineup
- Term insurance covers prime earning years cleanly
- Disability insurance protects your most valuable asset: income
- Umbrella coverage guards against big, unexpected losses
- Long seasons reward preparation, not optimism

Part III: Getting on Base (Investing Fundamentals)

Base Hits Win More Games Than Home Runs

Every baseball player learns this early, even if the highlights tell a different story.

Home runs are exciting. They bring the crowd to its feet. They show up on SportsCenter. But they are also rare. Most games are won by base hits, walks, smart situational hitting, and players who understand how to keep innings alive.

Championship teams are built on getting on base.

Investing works the same way.

The biggest mistake athletes make with money is chasing the financial equivalent of home runs. Hot stocks. Big bets. Fast money. Stories about someone who "made it" overnight. Those stories are loud, emotional, and tempting. They are also unreliable.

Wealth is built the way games are won. One base at a time.

Why Fundamentals Matter More Than Flash

In baseball, fundamentals are boring to outsiders.

Hitting the cutoff.

Moving runners over.

Taking a walk instead of forcing a swing.

Executing the same mechanics day after day.

No one puts these plays on a highlight reel. Coaches obsess over them because they win games.

Investing fundamentals work the same way.

Understanding how markets function. Knowing the difference between ownership and speculation. Building diversified positions. Staying invested through ups and downs. These actions do not feel exciting, but they create consistency.

Most athletes lose money not because they are reckless, but because they skip fundamentals and try to swing for the fences too early.

You do not build a batting average by swinging for home runs every at-bat. You build it by getting on base.

The Problem With Home-Run Investing

Home-run investing usually sounds like this:

"This stock is about to explode."

"This deal is guaranteed."

"This is how real money is made."

"If you don't get in now, you'll miss it."

These pitches create urgency and emotion. They also remove discipline.

In baseball terms, this is swinging at a pitch in the dirt because you are trying to do too much. Sometimes you get lucky. Most of the time, you strike out or ground into a double play.

Chasing home runs increases:

- Risk
- Volatility
- Emotional decision-making
- Inconsistency

And inconsistency kills long-term performance.

Getting on Base Financially

Getting on base financially means doing the basics well.

It looks like:

- Saving consistently
- Investing regularly
- Diversifying instead of concentrating
- Staying patient during slumps
- Letting time and compounding work

In baseball terms, this is quality at-bats. Fouling off tough pitches. Taking walks. Putting the ball in play. Making the defense work.

You are not trying to win the game in one swing. You are trying to stay in the inning.

Small wins compound. Base hits stack. Momentum builds.

Reps, Timing, and Discipline

Every hitter understands timing.

You cannot rush your swing. You cannot guess every pitch. You trust your mechanics and react.

Investing requires the same discipline.

You show up.

You invest consistently.

You do not overreact to short-term movement.

You stick to the approach even when results are quiet.

In baseball, a hitter who panics during a slump starts changing mechanics every at-bat. That only makes things worse. The same thing happens financially when investors constantly change strategies.

Discipline keeps you steady when emotions rise.

Coach's Perspective

A coach would keep this simple.

- **"Get on base."**
- **"Take the walk."**
- **"Don't chase."**
- **"Trust your swing."**
- **"Let the game come to you."**

Good teams do not beat themselves. Good investors do not either.

Winning the Long Game

No team wins a season on home runs alone.

They win by stacking base hits, protecting innings, and trusting the process. Investing fundamentals work the same way. They keep you in the game long enough for compounding to matter.

Base hits feel small in the moment.

They win championships over time.

Chapter 9: How Financial Markets Really Work

Every baseball player remembers the first time the game sped up. The pitcher's delivery felt quicker. The ball moved differently. Crowd noise blended into the background. At first, it felt chaotic. You were reacting instead of anticipating. Then, after enough reps, film, and at-bats, something changed. The game slowed down. You started recognizing patterns. You could tell what pitch was coming by the count, the grip, or the situation.

The game did not change. **You did.**

Financial markets work the same way.

To people on the outside, markets look random. Numbers flashing. Headlines screaming. Opinions everywhere. One day everything is up. The next day everything is down. It feels unpredictable and intimidating, especially if no one ever explained how it actually works.

But beneath the noise is a system.

And once you understand the system, the chaos starts to make sense.

How Financial Markets Function

At their core, financial markets are places where ownership and risk are exchanged.

Companies need money to grow. They need to hire employees, build products, expand facilities, and compete. Investors provide that capital in exchange for ownership or repayment with interest.

That is it.

Markets exist to connect businesses that need capital with people willing to provide it.

In baseball terms, the market is the league itself. Teams compete, rebuild, spend, cut costs, and adapt. Some teams dominate for stretches. Others struggle. But the league keeps moving forward season after season.

Markets are not designed to make you comfortable. They are designed to function.

Prices move based on expectations about the future, not just what happened yesterday. That is why markets can go down even when things look fine, or go up when headlines are negative. The scoreboard reflects expectations, not emotions.

Stocks, Bonds, and Ownership

Understanding what you actually own is critical.

Stocks represent ownership.

When you buy stock, you are buying a piece of a real business. That business sells products or services, pays employees, competes with rivals, and makes decisions that affect profitability.

When the business grows, your ownership becomes more valuable. When it struggles, your ownership feels the pain.

Bonds are loans.

When you buy a bond, you are lending money to a company or government. In return, you receive interest and the promise of your principal back later. Less upside. More predictability.

In baseball terms:

- Stocks are everyday position players. They drive offense and long-term success.
- Bonds are pitching and defense. They reduce volatility and protect the game.

You do not win championships with offense alone. You do not build wealth with growth alone. Balance matters.

Investing is not betting. It is owning productive assets and letting them work over time.

Market Cycles and Volatility

Markets move in cycles.

Growth.

Slowdown.

Correction.

Recovery.

Repeat.

This is not a flaw. It is normal.

Volatility is simply movement. Prices go up and down. That movement creates discomfort, especially for people who have not lived through many cycles.

In baseball terms, volatility is a slump.

Every hitter slumps. Every team goes through stretches where nothing falls. That does not mean the approach is broken. It means baseball is hard.

Athletes who panic during a slump start changing mechanics, guessing at pitches, and pressing. Investors do the same thing during market volatility. They abandon plans, sell at the wrong time, or chase whatever just worked.

The mistake is not volatility. The mistake is reacting emotionally to it.

Why Long-Term Strategy Beats Hot Streaks

Every season has hot streaks.

A hitter catches fire for three weeks.

A team wins ten straight.

A rookie bursts onto the scene.

The best players enjoy the streak but do not change who they are because of it. They know baseball always evens out.

Financial markets are full of hot streaks too.

A stock surges.

A sector explodes.

A new trend dominates headlines.

Chasing those streaks feels exciting. It also usually leads to buying high and selling low.

In baseball terms, this is chasing yesterday's performance. It is swinging harder because the last guy hit a home run. That mindset breaks discipline.

Long-term investing is about sustained drives, not highlight plays. It is about staying in position through full seasons, not winning one inning.

Why the Market Rewards Patience

The market rewards three things consistently:

- Ownership
- Time
- Discipline

You do not need to predict every move. You need to stay invested long enough for growth to matter. Businesses grow. Economies expand. Innovation continues. That progress shows up over decades, not days.

In baseball terms, this is trusting the season. One bad series does not define a year. One bad year does not define a career.

Athletes who understand long seasons handle slumps better. Investors who understand long timelines make fewer mistakes.

Coach's Perspective

What would your coach say?

- **"Trust the system."**
- **"Stay within yourself."**

- **"Don't chase."**
- **"One pitch at a time."**
- **"The film doesn't lie."**

Markets punish freelancing the same way baseball does. Discipline, preparation, and patience always win over emotion.

Game Situations and Decision Points

The market drops suddenly.

Do you panic and sell, or remember that cycles are normal?

You hear about a hot stock or trend.

Do you chase it, or evaluate whether it fits your plan?

You feel behind financially.

Do you force risk, or stay disciplined and let time work?

These moments mirror late-inning at-bats. Pressure reveals preparation.

Common Athlete Mistakes and Financial Parallels

Athletes press during slumps.

Financially, that leads to panic selling.

Athletes chase hot streaks.

Financially, that leads to buying hype.

Athletes abandon mechanics under pressure.

Financially, that leads to abandoning long-term strategy.

The same mistakes lose games and money.

Winning the Long Game

Markets reward people who stay in the game.

Not the smartest.

Not the boldest.

The most disciplined.

Understanding how markets actually work removes fear. It replaces reaction with confidence. Just like baseball, once the game slows down, execution improves.

You do not need to win every day.

You need to stay in the lineup.

Athlete Takeaways

- Markets are systems, not chaos
- Stocks mean ownership, not gambling
- Volatility is normal, not failure
- Hot streaks fade, discipline lasts
- Stay patient, trust the season, and keep showing up

Chapter 10: Risk, Return, and the Power of Compounding

Opening Story From Baseball

Every baseball player learns this lesson early.

You do not get better from one perfect swing. You get better from thousands of swings. Some good. Some bad. Some ugly. You show up every day, take reps, review film, make adjustments, and trust that progress will show up over time.

No hitter walks into spring training expecting to be in midseason form after one week. Strength builds slowly. Timing improves gradually. Confidence grows through repetition. Then, almost without noticing, the game feels easier.

Money works the same way.

Risk, return, and compounding are not separate ideas. They are connected. When you understand how they work together, small, consistent decisions turn into meaningful results. When you misunderstand them, impatience and fear derail progress before it ever has a chance to show up.

Risk and Reward Tradeoffs

There is no reward without risk.

In baseball, every decision carries tradeoffs. Swing aggressively and you might drive the ball into the gap, or you might strike out. Shorten up and put the ball in play, and you reduce strikeouts, but you also limit power. Coaches constantly balance these choices based on situation, count, and personnel.

Investing works the same way.

Higher potential returns usually come with higher risk. Lower-risk investments usually provide more stability but slower growth. There is no option that delivers maximum return with no risk. Anyone promising that is selling fantasy, not reality.

In baseball terms, this is approach at the plate. You do not swing for the fences every pitch. You adjust based on the count, the pitcher, and the game situation. Smart hitters know when to be aggressive and when to stay disciplined.

The goal is not to eliminate risk. The goal is to take **appropriate** risk for your situation.

Volatility vs Permanent Loss

This is where most people get tripped up.

Volatility is movement. Prices go up and down. That is normal.

Permanent loss is damage. It happens when money cannot recover.

Markets dropping is volatility.

Selling at the wrong time out of fear is permanent loss.

In baseball terms, volatility is an 0-for-4 night. Permanent loss is abandoning your swing mechanics because of one bad game.

Every hitter slumps. The ones who survive do not panic. They stick to fundamentals, trust their preparation, and let the numbers normalize over time.

Athletes often mistake discomfort for danger. Seeing red numbers feels bad, so it must be wrong. In reality, volatility is the cost of participation. You do not earn long-term returns without riding through short-term swings.

Permanent loss usually comes from:

- Panic selling
- Overleveraging
- Chasing hype
- Abandoning the plan under pressure

Those are mental mistakes, not market failures.

Compounding Over Time

Compounding is progress building on progress.

Your money earns returns. Those returns earn additional returns. Over time, the effect accelerates. Early progress feels slow. Later progress feels dramatic.

In baseball terms, compounding is cumulative reps.

One day in the cage does not change anything.

One week starts to feel better.

One year changes your swing.

Five years changes your career.

Compounding rewards consistency, not intensity. You do not need one massive win. You need steady participation over time.

This is why athletes who start early have such an advantage financially. Time does more work than effort ever could. You cannot replicate time later.

Why Compounding Feels Invisible at First

Compounding is deceptive because early results look small.

In the beginning:

- Account balances grow slowly

- Gains feel unimpressive
- Progress seems delayed

This is where most people quit.

In baseball terms, this is leaving early in the season because results are not immediate. The players who stay patient are the ones still standing in August and September.

Compounding works quietly. Then suddenly. The mistake is judging it too early.

The Real Cost of Waiting

Waiting feels safe.

Many athletes delay investing because they want more confidence, better timing, or more money. They tell themselves they will start later, when things are clearer.

The hidden cost is time.

Every year you wait is a year compounding cannot work for you. That lost time cannot be recovered.

In baseball terms, skipping offseason training puts you behind before the season even starts. You might feel rested, but everyone else is improving while you stand still.

You do not need to start big. You need to start now.

Why Athletes Are Actually Built for Compounding

Athletes already understand this mindset.

You trust reps.

You trust practice.

You trust long-term development.

You know progress is uneven.

You know effort compounds.

The challenge is translating that mindset from the field to money. Once you do, investing becomes less emotional and more familiar.

Compounding is not magic. It is discipline showing up over time.

Coach's Perspective

What would your coach say?

- **"Reps matter."**
- **"Trust the process."**
- **"Don't cheat the work."**
- **"Stack good days."**
- **"One at-bat at a time."**

Coaches do not promise instant results. They promise progress if you stay committed. Compounding works the same way.

Game Situations and Decision Points

The market drops.

Do you stop investing, or keep showing up like you would during a slump?

You feel behind financially.

Do you force risk, or trust that consistency will catch up?

You want to wait for the perfect moment.

Do you realize that waiting costs more than starting imperfectly?

These are season-defining decisions.

Common Athlete Mistakes and Financial Parallels

Athletes chase quick fixes.

Financially, that leads to over-risking.

Athletes skip fundamentals.

Financially, that leads to inconsistent investing.

Athletes expect immediate results.

Financially, that leads to quitting too early.

The same impatience that ruins development ruins compounding.

Winning the Long Game

Compounding does not reward brilliance. It rewards discipline.

You do not need to be perfect.

You need to be consistent.

You need to stay in the game.

Baseball careers are built over seasons. Financial success is built the same way. Trust the reps. Trust the time. Let progress do its work.

Athlete Takeaways

- Risk and reward are always connected
- Volatility is normal; panic causes permanent damage
- Compounding rewards reps, not hero swings
- Waiting costs more than starting small
- Stay disciplined, trust the process, and keep showing up

Chapter 11: Stocks Without the Highlight Reel

Opening Story From Baseball

Every player has seen this happen.

A hitter gets hot for a week. A couple of home runs. A few balls hit hard. Suddenly everyone is talking. The crowd buzzes when he walks to the plate. Teammates start saying things like, "This guy's locked in," or "He's figured it out."

Then the league adjusts.

Pitchers change their approach. Breaking balls show up earlier in the count. Fastballs disappear. The same hitter who looked unstoppable a week ago starts chasing pitches and pressing for results.

The highlight reel made it look easy. The reality was always harder.

Stocks work the same way.

Most people do not struggle with stocks because they are incapable. They struggle because they focus on highlights instead of fundamentals. Headlines. Hot names. Big swings. Quick wins. The noise hides what actually matters.

Winning with stocks is not about chasing moments. It is about understanding what you actually own and why.

What Owning Stock Actually Means

When you buy a stock, you are not buying a ticker symbol, a chart, or a headline.

You are buying ownership in a real business.

That business:

- Sells products or services
- Employs people
- Competes with other companies
- Faces good years and bad years
- Makes decisions that affect long-term results

In baseball terms, owning stock is being part of the organization, not just cheering from the stands. Your outcome depends on how the team performs over time, not one swing or one game.

This is where many athletes get tripped up.

They treat stocks like bets instead of ownership. If the price moves up quickly, they feel smart. If it drops, they feel like they failed. That mindset creates emotional decisions and poor timing.

Businesses grow slowly. Profits compound over time. Ownership rewards patience, not urgency.

Growth vs Value Investing

Growth and value are two common ways people talk about stocks.

Growth investing focuses on companies expected to grow faster than average. These companies often reinvest profits, expand aggressively, and attract attention. They usually look exciting. They also tend to be more volatile.

Value investing focuses on companies priced lower relative to fundamentals like earnings, cash flow, or assets. These companies may be boring. They may not dominate headlines. But they often provide steady performance.

In baseball terms, growth stocks are power hitters. They can change the game with one swing, but they strike out more often. Value stocks are contact hitters. They may not lead the highlight reel, but they get on base consistently.

Championship teams need both.

A lineup full of power hitters struggles when timing is off. A lineup with only contact hitters lacks punch. Balance matters.

Financially, relying entirely on one style creates risk. Growth can stall. Value can lag. Owning a mix reduces pressure and smooths results.

Dividends and Total Return

Dividends are cash payments some companies make to shareholders. They provide income while you own the stock.

But dividends are only part of the story.

Total return includes:

- Price growth
- Dividends received

Focusing on only one misses the full picture.

In baseball terms, home runs matter, but so do walks, singles, and advancing runners. The scoreboard reflects everything, not just the loudest plays.

Some companies pay no dividends because they reinvest everything back into growth. Others pay steady dividends and grow slowly. Neither approach is automatically better. The right mix depends on goals, time horizon, and need for income.

Athletes often gravitate toward dividends because they feel tangible. Cash feels real. That is understandable. But ignoring growth potential can limit long-term outcomes.

Total return is the full season, not one stat.

Why Stock Prices Move the Way They Do

Stock prices do not move based only on today's results.

They move based on expectations about the future.

Earnings forecasts. Industry trends. Competition. Interest rates. Investor sentiment. All of it matters.

In baseball terms, this is scouting reports and projections. A prospect's value changes before he ever steps on the field based on expectations. Veterans decline in value before performance collapses.

Markets are forward-looking. That is why prices sometimes move in ways that feel disconnected from reality. The market is not reacting to today's box score. It is reacting to tomorrow's forecast.

Understanding this helps athletes stay composed when prices move unexpectedly.

Common Stock Market Myths Athletes Hear

Locker rooms and group chats are full of stock myths.

"You have to trade constantly to win."

"You need inside information."

"If the price drops, you failed."

"Stocks are just gambling."

These ideas sound confident. They are wrong.

Trading constantly usually increases mistakes and taxes. Inside information is illegal and unnecessary. Price drops are part of ownership. Stocks are not gambling when they represent diversified ownership over time.

In baseball terms, this is freelancing instead of trusting the system. One flashy play might work. Over time, it breaks discipline and leads to errors.

Why Highlight Investing Fails

Highlight investing is chasing what just worked.

The stock that doubled.

The company everyone is talking about.

The story that sounds unstoppable.

This approach feels exciting. It is also dangerous.

By the time something becomes obvious, much of the opportunity is already priced in. Expectations are high. Mistakes get punished harder.

In baseball terms, this is swinging at the first pitch because the last guy hit a home run. It ignores context and leads to weak contact.

Winning investors focus on fundamentals, diversification, and time. Not highlights.

Coach's Perspective

What would your coach say?

- **"Make the simple play."**
- **"Do your job."**
- **"Stop trying to be the hero."**
- **"Trust the system."**
- **"The scoreboard doesn't lie."**

Coaches hate freelancing because it breaks structure. Stocks reward the same discipline. Fundamentals win over flash.

Game Situations and Decision Points

A stock drops after bad news.

Do you panic, or remember you own a business, not a headline?

You hear about a hot stock everyone is buying.

Do you chase it, or evaluate whether it fits your plan?

Your portfolio feels boring.

Do you add excitement, or trust that boring often means working?

These are season-long decisions, not one-game choices.

Common Athlete Mistakes and Financial Parallels

Athletes chase highlights.

Financially, that becomes hype investing.

Athletes abandon fundamentals under pressure.

Financially, that becomes panic selling.

Athletes overestimate instincts.

Financially, that becomes ignoring diversification.

The same habits that lose games lose money.

Winning the Long Game

Stocks are not lottery tickets.

They are ownership stakes in productive businesses. When used correctly, they build wealth slowly and steadily. When used emotionally, they create stress and regret.

Baseball careers are not built on one swing. Financial success is not built on one stock. The long game rewards patience, balance, and discipline.

Trust the process. Ignore the highlight reel.

Athlete Takeaways

- Owning stock means owning a real business
- Growth and value both matter over a full season
- Dividends plus price growth equal total return
- Headlines and hype are not a strategy
- Fundamentals, patience, and balance win the long game

Chapter 12: Bonds and Playing Solid Defense

Every championship team has this in common.

They play defense.

Not the flashy kind that makes highlight reels, but the steady kind that turns singles into outs, limits extra bases, and keeps games from spiraling. Great defensive teams do not always get credit when things are going well. But when pressure hits, when the game tightens in the late innings, defense is what keeps you in position to win.

Pitchers love knowing the defense is solid behind them. It allows them to stay aggressive without fear that one mistake will unravel the entire game.

Bonds play that same role in a financial plan.

They are not exciting. They do not generate buzz. They rarely show up in conversations about big wins. But when markets get chaotic, bonds are often the difference between staying composed and panicking.

Defense does not win games by itself.

But without it, you lose them.

How Bonds Work

At their core, bonds are simple.

A bond is a loan.

When you buy a bond, you are lending money to a government or a company. In exchange, they agree to:

- Pay you interest on a regular schedule
- Return your original investment, called principal, at a specific date known as maturity

That structure is intentional. Bonds are designed to be predictable.

In baseball terms, bonds are your defensive alignment. They are not swinging for the fences. They are positioned to reduce damage and keep the game under control.

Stocks represent ownership and growth.

Bonds represent stability and income.

Both matter. They just serve different purposes.

Many athletes misunderstand bonds because they compare them to stocks and feel disappointed by the lack of excitement. That is like judging a shortstop by home runs instead of fielding percentage. You are measuring the wrong thing.

Why Bonds Are Often Overlooked

Bonds do not feel rewarding in the short term.

They move slowly.

They do not double overnight.

They do not dominate headlines.

In a culture obsessed with offense and power, defense gets ignored until it fails.

Financially, this leads many athletes to overexpose themselves to risk early. They load up on growth and assume they will "figure out defense later." Sometimes that works. Sometimes one bad stretch erases years of progress.

Bonds exist to reduce volatility and provide balance. They are not there to impress. They are there to protect.

Interest Rate Risk and Credit Risk

Not all bonds are the same.

Two primary risks matter when owning bonds.

Interest rate risk

Bond prices move when interest rates change. When rates rise, existing bonds become less attractive, and their prices fall. When rates fall, existing bonds become more valuable.

Credit risk

This is the risk that the borrower cannot repay the loan. Governments and strong companies usually carry lower credit risk. Weaker borrowers offer higher interest to compensate for higher risk.

In baseball terms, this is field positioning and trust.

You do not play everyone at the same depth. You adjust based on the hitter, the count, and the situation. Strong pitchers can challenge hitters. Riskier situations require caution.

Higher interest payments often look attractive. They usually come with higher risk. That risk tends to show up during stress, not during calm periods.

Understanding risk allows bonds to play the role they are supposed to play.

When Bonds Make Sense

Bonds make the most sense when stability matters.

That often includes:

- When you are closer to using the money
- When income is needed
- When volatility would cause emotional mistakes
- When preserving progress matters more than maximizing growth

In baseball terms, this is protecting a late-inning lead. You do not swing for a three-run homer when one run wins the game. You play smart. You reduce mistakes. You shorten the game.

Younger athletes often dismiss bonds because time feels abundant. Older athletes wish they had respected defense earlier.

The point is not age. The point is timeline.

If you cannot afford a big drawdown at the wrong time, bonds help protect against it.

Bonds as Emotional Stabilizers

One of the most overlooked benefits of bonds is emotional control.

When part of your portfolio behaves predictably, it becomes easier to stay disciplined during market downturns. Not everything is moving at once. Not everything feels out of control.

In baseball terms, this is a reliable defense calming the pitcher. When you trust what is behind you, you execute better out front.

Bonds help investors stay invested in stocks during rough periods. They reduce the urge to panic, sell at the wrong time, or abandon the plan entirely.

That emotional benefit often matters more than the return itself.

Stability in a Diversified Portfolio

Diversification is not about maximizing returns.

It is about managing risk.

A well-balanced portfolio includes:

- Stocks for growth
- Bonds for stability
- Cash for flexibility

In baseball terms, this is complementary baseball. Pitching, defense, and offense working together. Remove one piece and the system breaks down.

A portfolio made entirely of stocks relies on everything going right. A portfolio with balance is built to survive when things go wrong.

Bonds act as ballast. They keep the ship steady in rough water.

Why Balanced Portfolios Feel Boring

Balanced portfolios often feel dull.

Some years stocks lead.

Some years bonds hold things together.

Nothing feels dramatic.

That boredom is a feature, not a flaw.

In baseball terms, clean defense rarely makes headlines. But it keeps you competitive every night. Sloppy defense turns small mistakes into big innings.

If your portfolio feels boring, it is probably doing its job.

Avoiding the "All Offense" Trap

Many athletes fall into extremes.

All growth when markets are rising.

All cash when markets feel scary.

That behavior increases stress and damages results.

In baseball terms, this is constantly changing lineups and defensive schemes based on yesterday's outcome. Confidence disappears. Execution suffers.

Bonds reduce the need for extreme reactions. They allow you to stay consistent instead of swinging wildly between strategies.

Coach's Perspective

What would your coach say?

- **"Protect the lead."**
- **"Do not beat yourself."**

- **"Play clean defense."**
- **"Win the little things."**
- **"Stay disciplined."**

No coach builds a team with offense alone. Control wins championships.

Bonds are about control.

Game Situations and Decision Points

Markets become volatile.

Do you lean on balance or chase offense?

You are approaching a major financial goal.

Do you protect progress or keep swinging big?

Your portfolio feels boring.

Do you understand why that might be a good sign?

Defense shows up when pressure hits.

Common Athlete Mistakes and Financial Parallels

Athletes ignore defense.

Financially, that means ignoring bonds.

Athletes chase excitement.

Financially, that means excess risk.

Athletes misunderstand roles.

Financially, that means poor allocation.

Awareness corrects all three.

Winning the Long Game

Bonds do not win games by themselves.

They help you avoid losing them.

Defense keeps you in position to win. Bonds keep your financial plan intact when conditions change. Long-term success is not about constant offense. It is about staying upright, composed, and disciplined.

That is how seasons are won.

Athlete Takeaways

- Bonds are loans designed for stability, not excitement
- Interest rate and credit risk matter more than yield
- Bonds make sense when preserving progress matters
- Balance reduces volatility and emotional mistakes
- Solid defense keeps you in the game all season

Chapter 13: Funds, ETFs, and Team-Based Investing

No championship team is built around one player.

Even the greatest hitters in the game need protection in the lineup. They need someone to get on base ahead of them. Someone to drive them in behind them. Pitchers need catchers. Infielders need outfielders. Depth matters over a 162-game season.

Baseball punishes teams that rely on one star or one strategy. Injuries happen. Slumps happen. Long seasons expose weak rosters fast.

Investing works the same way.

Funds and ETFs are team-based investing. Instead of relying on one company, one idea, or one hot streak, you own a lineup of investments working together. That teamwork reduces mistakes, smooths performance, and increases the odds that you stay competitive over time.

You are not trying to hit a home run every at-bat.

You are trying to build a roster that wins series after series.

Why Team-Based Investing Matters

Many athletes are drawn to individual stocks because they feel familiar.

You recognize the brand.

You hear the story.

You feel connected to the name.

That is like building a team by drafting only sluggers because home runs are exciting.

It looks good on paper.

It falls apart over a long season.

Team-based investing accepts a simple truth. You do not need to be right about everything. You need to stay in the game long enough for discipline and consistency to matter.

Funds and ETFs help you do that.

Mutual Funds vs ETFs

Both mutual funds and ETFs pool money from many investors and invest it across a group of stocks or bonds. The goal is diversification and professional management or structured exposure.

The differences are structural, not philosophical.

Mutual Funds

- Typically trade once per day after the market closes
- Often actively managed
- May require minimum investments
- Can distribute taxable gains during the year

ETFs (Exchange-Traded Funds)

- Trade throughout the day like stocks
- Often follow indexes
- Usually have lower costs
- Tend to be more tax efficient

In baseball terms, mutual funds are structured practices. Everything runs on a set schedule. ETFs are game-speed reps. You see movement throughout the day.

Both can work.

What matters is not which one sounds better. What matters is how they fit your system, your discipline, and your ability to execute consistently.

Index vs Active Investing

This is one of the most misunderstood debates in investing.

Index investing aims to match the performance of a market or segment. No heroics. No predictions. Just exposure to the system as it exists.

Active investing tries to outperform through selection, timing, and judgment.

Neither approach is inherently right or wrong.

In baseball terms, index investing is running the base offense. You know the plays. You know the spacing. You trust the system to work over time.

Active investing is calling audibles. Sometimes it works beautifully. Sometimes it leads to confusion and blown assignments.

Audibles require:

- Skill
- Discipline
- Consistency
- Emotional control

Most athletes do better sticking to the system rather than trying to outsmart the game every possession. Index investing rewards patience and consistency. Active investing rewards execution and restraint, not confidence alone.

The mistake is assuming activity equals progress.

Why Index Investing Fits Athletes Well

Athletes already understand systems.

You know how to follow a game plan.

You know how to trust reps.

You know how consistency beats talent when talent gets lazy.

Index investing aligns with that mindset.

You are not betting on one hitter.

You are betting on the league.

Over time, businesses grow, innovate, and replace weaker players. Indexes adjust automatically. You are not making lineup changes every week. The system does it for you.

That is powerful.

Fees and Expense Ratios

Fees are the silent opponent.

They do not show up in highlight reels.

They do not feel dramatic.

They quietly drain performance year after year.

Expense ratios are the cost of running a fund. They may look small, but over decades they compound just like returns.

In baseball terms, fees are unforced errors.

One error does not lose a game.

A lot of them lose seasons.

Lower fees mean more of your return stays on your team instead of going to management. This is why simple, low-cost funds often outperform more complex strategies over time.

You do not need the fanciest system.

You need the one that does not beat itself.

Diversification Without Complexity

Diversification means spreading risk across many investments.

It does not mean owning everything.

It does not mean constant tinkering.

It does not mean chasing balance every day.

It means coverage.

In baseball terms, diversification is roster construction. You do not ask one player to play every position. You assign roles and trust coverage.

Funds and ETFs allow you to diversify without managing dozens of individual investments. That reduces stress, mistakes, and emotional decision-making.

Simple diversification done consistently beats complex strategies done inconsistently.

Why Complexity Hurts Execution

Athletes often believe complexity equals sophistication.

In reality, complexity usually breaks down under pressure.

The more moving parts you have:

- The harder it is to stay disciplined
- The easier it is to panic
- The more likely you are to abandon the plan

Baseball teams simplify when the game gets tight. They focus on fundamentals. Clean execution wins close games.

Investing is no different.

Funds exist to simplify execution so you can focus on behavior instead of constantly managing decisions.

Coach's Perspective

What would your coach say?

- **"Do your job."**
- **"Trust the system."**
- **"We over me."**
- **"Protect the locker room."**
- **"Don't try to do too much."**
- **"Win the little things."**

Team-based investing removes ego. You are not trying to be right. You are trying to stay consistent.

That mindset wins seasons.

Game Situations and Decision Points

You want excitement.

Do you pick individual stocks or build a team?

You see a fund with higher returns.

Do you understand the fees and risk?

You feel behind.

Do you complicate the plan or stick to fundamentals?

The same pressures show up in investing as they do in baseball. The response determines outcomes.

Common Athlete Mistakes and Financial Parallels

Athletes try to carry the team alone.

Financially, that means concentrated bets.

Athletes ignore fundamentals.

Financially, that means high fees and poor diversification.

Athletes chase stars.

Financially, that means hype investing.

Championship teams avoid these traps.

Winning the Long Game

Team-based investing works because it respects reality.

Seasons are long.

Slumps happen.

Injuries happen.

Markets change.

Funds and ETFs give you depth. They allow you to stay invested without needing to be perfect. Over time, discipline compounds.

You do not need to win every inning.

You need to stay competitive all season.

Athlete Takeaways

- Funds and ETFs are team-based investing, not solo plays
- Index strategies reward discipline and consistency
- Fees compound just like returns, protect both
- Diversification reduces mistakes and stress
- Simple systems outperform complicated ones over a long season

Chapter 14: Real Estate and Alternative Plays

Opening Story From Baseball

Every team has specialty packages.

A bunt defense.

A hit-and-run.

A late-inning matchup brought in from the bullpen.

These plays exist for a reason. When used at the right moment, by the right players, in the right situation, they can change a game. But no coach installs specialty plays before the team can handle the basics. If players do not understand fundamentals, timing, and assignments, those plays turn into disasters.

Real estate and alternative investments work the same way.

They are not the foundation of most financial plans. They are situational tools. When used intentionally, they can strengthen a long-term strategy. When used too early, too aggressively, or without understanding, they create risk instead of results.

Athletes often get drawn to these plays because they sound advanced. The mistake is running them before the fundamentals are solid.

Why Athletes Are Drawn to Real Estate and Alternatives

Athletes are trained to look for edges.

Extra reps.

Better equipment.

A competitive advantage.

That mindset is powerful. It is also why real estate and alternatives are so appealing. They are often marketed as the "next level" of investing.

You hear phrases like:

- "This is how real money is made."
- "Stocks are too slow."
- "You need multiple income streams."
- "Wealthy people don't do it the simple way."

Those statements are not always wrong. They are often mistimed.

In baseball terms, this is calling a hit-and-run because you are bored with singles. Sometimes it works. Sometimes it leads to an easy out and a frustrated dugout.

Specialty plays are about timing, not ego.

Renting vs Owning

Owning property is often treated like a milestone. Renting is sometimes framed as falling behind.

That framing is wrong.

Renting provides flexibility.

Owning provides stability and long-term commitment.

Neither choice is a trophy. Neither is a failure.

Renting is like being on a one-year contract. You can relocate. You are not responsible for repairs. You preserve flexibility if income changes, opportunities arise, or life shifts unexpectedly.

Owning is like signing a long-term deal. You build equity. You control your environment. You also commit to maintenance, taxes, insurance, and long-term costs.

The right choice depends on:

- Income stability
- Career mobility
- Location
- Time horizon
- Willingness to manage responsibility

Buying before you are ready is like committing to a system that does not fit your roster. The playbook may look good, but execution suffers under pressure.

The Hidden Costs of Ownership

Many athletes focus on the upside of owning property and underestimate the responsibility.

Ownership includes:

- Maintenance and repairs
- Property taxes
- Insurance
- Unexpected expenses
- Reduced flexibility
- Time and attention

In baseball terms, this is playing through an injury without depth behind you. You might manage for a while, but every mistake hurts more.

Real estate can be a powerful tool when it fits. When it does not, it becomes an anchor that limits options.

REITs and Indirect Ownership

REITs (Real Estate Investment Trusts) allow you to invest in real estate without owning property directly.

You get exposure to:

- Rental income
- Commercial properties
- Real estate growth

Without:

- Tenants
- Toilets
- Leverage management
- Maintenance calls

In baseball terms, REITs are like being part of the organization without running day-to-day operations. You benefit from the system without carrying the full load.

REITs can:

- Provide income
- Add diversification
- Preserve liquidity
- Reduce operational stress

They still carry market risk. Prices fluctuate. Income can change. They are not guaranteed.

For many athletes, REITs make more sense early than direct property ownership because they keep the system simple and flexible.

Alternatives Like Commodities and Private Investments

Alternatives include:

- Commodities
- Private equity
- Private credit
- Hedge-style strategies
- Other non-traditional assets

They can add diversification. They can also add complexity.

Most alternatives are:

- Illiquid
- Expensive
- Hard to value
- Difficult to exit
- Less transparent

In baseball terms, these are trick plays.

They can change momentum when timed perfectly. When forced, they create turnovers.

Alternatives are rarely bad on their own. They are bad when used without a foundation or without understanding the downside.

Why Alternatives Are Often Overused

Alternatives appeal to ego.

They feel sophisticated.

They sound exclusive.

They promise access and advantage.

That appeal leads people to use them before they are ready.

In baseball terms, this is installing trick plays before players understand base assignments. When pressure hits, confusion shows up fast.

Alternatives should complement a strong foundation. They should not replace it.

Liquidity and Risk Considerations

Liquidity is how quickly you can access your money.

Stocks and bonds are generally liquid.

Real estate and many alternatives are not.

When money is illiquid:

- Selling takes time
- Prices may be unfavorable
- Options shrink
- Stress increases

In baseball terms, this is field position. You cannot always reverse field. You cannot always escape pressure.

Before committing to illiquid investments, ask:

- When might I need this money?
- What happens if income changes?
- What if life forces an adjustment?
- Can I stay disciplined if access is limited?

Ignoring liquidity is one of the fastest ways athletes get trapped financially.

Why Liquidity Equals Flexibility

Flexibility creates options.

Options reduce stress.

Stress leads to mistakes.

Illiquid investments can be powerful when planned correctly. They can also create pressure when life changes unexpectedly.

Strong teams value flexibility. Strong financial plans do too.

You want to be able to adjust when the season does not go as planned.

Coach's Perspective

What would your coach say?

- **"Master the basics first."**
- **"Know the situation."**
- **"Don't force specialty plays."**
- **"Protect flexibility."**
- **"Do not beat yourself."**

Specialty investments belong in the right moment, not because they sound impressive.

Game Situations and Decision Points

You want to buy property.

Do you understand the full commitment, or just the upside?

You hear about a private deal.

Do you understand liquidity and risk, or just the return?

You feel bored with steady progress.

Do you add complexity, or stay disciplined?

Timing matters more than excitement.

Common Athlete Mistakes and Financial Parallels

Athletes rush into new roles.

Financially, that means premature complexity.

Athletes underestimate recovery time.

Financially, that means liquidity problems.

Athletes chase excitement.

Financially, that means unnecessary risk.

Championship teams avoid forcing plays.

Winning the Long Game

Real estate and alternatives are not shortcuts.

They are tools.

When used intentionally, they can strengthen a plan. When used emotionally, they create imbalance.

The goal is not to collect assets.

The goal is to build a system that holds up when pressure hits.

Master the basics first. Layer complexity only when it fits.

Athlete Takeaways

- Renting and owning serve different roles at different times
- REITs offer real estate exposure without operational burden
- Alternatives add complexity and require discipline
- Liquidity equals flexibility under pressure
- Master fundamentals before calling specialty plays

Part IV: Managing the Season

Winning is about adjustments, not ego.

Every baseball season is a grind.

One hundred sixty-two games. Hot streaks. Slumps. Injuries. Travel. Weather. Opponents who adjust after seeing you once. No team runs the exact same game plan from Opening Day to the final out. The teams that last are not the ones with the most talent on paper. They are the ones that adjust without panic and correct without ego.

Money works the same way.

A financial plan is not something you set once and never touch again. Income changes. Goals shift. Families grow. Careers take unexpected turns. Markets move. Life happens. Managing your finances is not about being perfect. It is about staying engaged and making smart adjustments as conditions change.

This part of the book is about learning how to manage the season, not just start it.

In baseball, the best players constantly evaluate what is working and what is not. They watch film. They adjust swing paths. They refine mechanics. They make small changes instead of blowing everything up after a bad week. Financial success requires the same maturity.

Ego is the enemy of good adjustments.

Ego says, "I don't need to look at this."

Ego says, "I already know what I'm doing."

Ego says, "I'll fix it later."

Adjustments require humility. You have to be willing to admit when something is not working and make changes without feeling like you failed. A slump does not mean you abandon your swing. A bad month financially does not mean you abandon your plan. It means you tighten fundamentals and stay disciplined.

Managing the season means understanding that progress is uneven.

There will be times when money feels easy. Income is strong. Expenses feel manageable. Markets cooperate. That is when complacency creeps in. Teams lose focus when things are going well. Financially, that shows up as lifestyle creep, unnecessary risk, and ignoring the details.

There will also be times when money feels tight. Unexpected expenses show up. Markets drop. Income slows. That is when panic leads to mistakes. Just like pressing at the plate, financial pressure can cause rushed decisions that make things worse.

Great teams stay composed in both situations.

They do not overreact to success.

They do not collapse under adversity.

They stay within the system and make smart, measured adjustments.

This part of the book focuses on how to do that with money.

You will learn how to:

- Build a lineup that fits your stage of life
- Trust a long-term strategy instead of chasing short-term results
- Make adjustments without over-managing
- Handle emotional pressure when things are not going your way

Managing the season also means accepting responsibility. No coach can swing the bat for you. No advisor can care more than you do. You are the one in the box. The goal is not to eliminate mistakes. The goal is to avoid compounding them through ego-driven decisions.

Baseball teaches patience.

You cannot fix everything in one at-bat.

You cannot judge a season by one series.

You win by stacking quality innings over time.

Money rewards the same approach.

Stay engaged.

Stay honest.

Make adjustments.

Protect the long-term plan.

That is how you manage the season and give yourself a chance to finish strong.

Chapter 15: Asset Allocation and Building the Lineup

Every baseball coach builds a lineup with intention.

You do not stack nine power hitters and hope for the best. You balance contact hitters, power, speed, defense, and situational roles. You think about who sets the table, who drives in runs, who protects the lineup, and who closes games late. The best lineups are not built around one star. They are built to win over a long season.

Asset allocation works the same way.

Asset allocation is how you build your financial lineup. It is the mix of stocks, bonds, and cash you choose to own and how those pieces work together. Just like baseball, the goal is not to dominate one inning. The goal is to score consistently, limit damage, and stay competitive through ups and downs.

Stocks, Bonds, and Cash Balance

Stocks, bonds, and cash each play a different role, just like players on the field.

Stocks are your everyday starters. They drive long-term growth. They create runs over time. They will strike out sometimes, but over a full season, they are responsible for most of the offense.

Bonds are your defense and bullpen. They provide stability. They slow the game down when things get chaotic. They are not there to steal headlines.

They are there to protect leads and reduce volatility.

Cash is your bench and your flexibility. It does not generate much return, but it gives you options. Cash allows you to handle injuries, weather delays, and extra innings without panicking.

A lineup with no power struggles to score. A lineup with no defense collapses late. A lineup with no bench options gets exposed when something goes wrong. Financially, too much emphasis on any one asset creates imbalance.

Asset allocation is about balance, not perfection.

Domestic vs International Exposure

Every baseball team plays more than one opponent.

You face different pitchers, different ballparks, different styles of play. If you only know how to hit one type of pitching, you get exposed quickly. Smart teams prepare for variety.

Financially, that is where domestic and international investing come in.

Domestic investments focus on companies based in your home country. International investments give you exposure to companies and economies around the world. Each behaves differently at different times.

Sometimes the home team dominates.

Sometimes international markets outperform.

Sometimes both struggle.

Sometimes one stabilizes the other.

In baseball terms, this is learning to hit both fastballs and off-speed pitches. You do not know which one is coming next, but you want a lineup that can handle both.

International exposure is not about predicting which country will win. It is about acknowledging that the global economy does not move in one direction at one speed. Diversification across regions reduces dependence on a single outcome.

Diversification Principles

Diversification is often misunderstood.

It does not mean owning everything.

It does not mean complexity.

It does not mean constant changes.

Diversification means spreading risk so one bad outcome does not ruin the season.

In baseball, diversification is having multiple ways to score. Singles, doubles, walks, stolen bases, sacrifice flies. When the home runs disappear, the team can still compete.

Financially, diversification spreads your investments across different companies, industries, asset types, and regions. The goal is not to eliminate losses. The goal is to avoid catastrophic losses.

Diversification works best when:

- Assets respond differently to the same event
- No single position dominates the lineup
- The plan is maintained through good and bad stretches

Diversification feels boring when things are going well. It feels essential when things are not.

Career-Stage Allocation

Lineups change over time.

A rebuilding team looks different than a championship contender. A veteran roster manages innings differently than a young team with energy to spare. The season dictates the strategy.

Your asset allocation should change as your career and life evolve.

Early career is about growth and flexibility. Time is on your side. You can tolerate more swings because you have more seasons ahead. Stocks usually play a larger role. Cash protects flexibility. Bonds may play a smaller supporting role.

Mid-career is about balance. Income may be higher, but responsibilities grow. Families, homes, and long-term goals matter more. Asset allocation often shifts toward stability without abandoning growth.

Later career is about protection and income. The focus shifts from building to sustaining. Bonds and cash become more important. Volatility matters more because there is less time to recover from big losses.

There is no universal perfect allocation. There is only what fits your current season.

Trying to run a rebuilding strategy in the late innings leads to mistakes. Playing not to lose in the first inning limits opportunity. Smart allocation matches the moment.

Coach's Perspective

A coach would not overthink this.

Build a balanced lineup.

Know your personnel.

Do not ask one player to do everything.

Adjust as the season changes.

Protect the long game.

Asset allocation is not about predicting the future. It is about preparing for it.

Game Situations and Decision Points

You feel confident and want more offense. Do you add risk without considering defense?

Markets are volatile. Do you abandon growth entirely or rebalance thoughtfully?

Your life changes. New job, family, or responsibility. Do you adjust the lineup or ignore the shift?

These are managerial decisions. Good managers stay engaged.

Common Athlete Mistakes and Financial Parallels

Athletes rely too much on one strength.

Financially, that means overconcentration.

Athletes ignore defense when offense feels good.

Financially, that means skipping stability.

Athletes refuse to adjust roles.

Financially, that means outdated allocations.

Winning the Long Game

Great teams do not win because of one lineup card. They win because they adjust without ego and stay committed to balance.

Asset allocation is how you stay competitive through an entire financial season. It is not about avoiding losses. It is about surviving them and continuing to score.

Build a lineup that fits your game.

Adjust as the season changes.

Protect your ability to stay in the game.

Athlete Takeaways

- Build a balanced lineup. Offense, defense, and flexibility all matter.
- Diversification keeps one bad stretch from ending the season.
- Domestic and international exposure prepare you for different opponents.
- Your lineup should evolve as your career and life evolve.
- Winning financially is about managing the season, not chasing one big inning.

Chapter 16: Buying, Holding, and Trusting the Process

Every baseball season tests patience.

You can do everything right and still go 0 for 4. You can hit the ball hard and find gloves. You can start hot and cool off. Great players do not panic after one bad series. They trust their mechanics, stick to their routine, and let the season play out.

Investing works the same way.

Buying, holding, and trusting the process sounds simple. It is simple. It is not easy. The difficulty is not the mechanics. The difficulty is emotion. Fear. Greed. Noise. Pressure to do something when the smartest move is often to stay disciplined.

This chapter is about learning to act like a professional, not a fan, when it comes to money.

Opening and Funding Accounts

Before you ever worry about market performance, you need access to the field.

That means opening the right accounts and funding them consistently.

Investment accounts are your stadium. If you are not on the field, you cannot score. Too many athletes overthink this step and delay for months or years waiting for the perfect setup. Professionals start with what is available and improve over time.

Common investment accounts include:

- Employer retirement plans like 401(k)s
- Individual retirement accounts such as Traditional or Roth IRAs
- Taxable brokerage accounts

Each account has rules, benefits, and tradeoffs. You do not need to master them all at once. You need to open the ones that fit your current situation and start contributing.

In baseball terms, this is getting into the lineup. You cannot worry about batting average if you never step into the box.

Funding accounts consistently matters more than timing the market. Automatic contributions remove decision making. Just like showing up to daily batting practice, consistency compounds.

Market Orders vs Limit Orders

Once you are in the game, you have to understand how orders work.

A market order means you buy or sell at the current market price. It prioritizes execution. You get in the game immediately.

A limit order means you set a specific price you are willing to pay or receive. It prioritizes price, not speed.

In baseball terms, a market order is swinging at a good pitch in the zone. A limit order is sitting on a specific pitch and location.

Both have a place.

Market orders are often appropriate for long-term investors buying diversified funds. The exact price on that day matters far less than time in the market.

Limit orders can make sense for individual stocks or situations where price discipline matters.

The mistake athletes make is overthinking this step. They obsess over pennies while missing years of growth. Execution matters more than perfection.

Do not confuse being precise with being productive.

Buy-and-Hold Discipline

This is where championships are won.

Buy-and-hold investing means you buy quality investments and hold them through good and bad periods. You do not jump in and out based on headlines, emotions, or short-term performance.

In baseball terms, buy-and-hold is trusting your swing. You do not rebuild your mechanics after every strikeout. You trust the work you put in during the offseason.

Markets move.

Prices fluctuate.

News cycles change daily.

Businesses, however, grow over years.

Buy-and-hold works because it aligns with how wealth is actually created. Ownership plus time plus discipline.

Athletes often struggle with this because they are competitive and used to reacting quickly. Investing rewards patience, not urgency.

The biggest gains often come after the hardest stretches. Selling during downturns locks in losses. Staying invested allows recovery to do its job.

Just like slumps do not define careers, downturns do not define long-term investors unless you quit.

Avoiding Emotional Decisions

Emotion is the toughest opponent you will face.

Fear shows up when markets drop.

Greed shows up when everyone else is making money.

Ego shows up when you want to prove you are smarter than the system.

These emotions are normal. Acting on them is optional.

Emotion-driven investing looks like:

- Selling after losses to stop the pain
- Chasing hot stocks or trends
- Constantly changing strategies
- Abandoning a plan during volatility

In baseball terms, this is swinging out of frustration. Pressing. Trying to hit a five-run homer instead of taking the single the defense gives you.

Emotional decisions usually feel urgent. Smart decisions feel boring.

Systems beat emotions. Automatic contributions, diversified portfolios, and clear rules remove the need to make decisions under pressure.

Professionals rely on routines. Fans rely on feelings.

Coach's Perspective

A coach would say it clearly.

Trust your training.

Stick to the plan.

Do not chase results.

Control what you can control.

Next pitch.

Buying and holding is not passive. It is disciplined. It is choosing not to react when reaction is tempting.

Game Situations and Decision Points

The market drops sharply. Do you sell to avoid further losses or keep executing the plan?

A friend tells you about a hot investment. Do you abandon your strategy or evaluate calmly?

You feel behind financially. Do you force risk or increase consistency?

These are high-pressure moments. How you respond matters more than what happens next.

Common Athlete Mistakes and Financial Parallels

Athletes panic during slumps.

Financially, that means selling at the worst time.

Athletes chase highlights.

Financially, that means chasing trends.

Athletes abandon fundamentals.

Financially, that means changing strategies constantly.

The same behaviors that lose games lose money.

Winning the Long Game

Baseball seasons are long for a reason. The best teams separate themselves through consistency, not streaks.

Financial success works the same way.

You do not need to be perfect.

You do not need to predict the market.

You do not need to react to every headline.

You need a plan you can execute.

You need the discipline to stick with it.

You need patience to let time work.

Trusting the process is not passive hope. It is active discipline repeated over years.

That is how professionals win.

Athlete Takeaways

- Open the account and get on the field. Delaying costs more than mistakes.
- Consistent funding beats perfect timing.
- Buy-and-hold is trusting your swing through slumps.
- Emotion is the toughest opponent. Systems keep it in check.
- Stay disciplined, play the long season, and let time do the work.

Chapter 17: Rebalancing and Mid-Season Adjustments

Every baseball season reaches a point where reality sets in.

What you thought you had in April is not exactly what you have in July. A starter is struggling. A reliever is overperforming. A rookie forces his way into the lineup. Injuries happen. Matchups change. Good teams do not panic when this happens. They adjust.

They do not blow up the roster every week.

They do not chase every hot streak.

They make thoughtful, disciplined adjustments that keep the team aligned with its long-term goal of winning over a full season.

That is exactly what rebalancing is in investing.

Rebalancing is not about predicting the future. It is about restoring discipline after the game has moved things out of alignment.

How Often to Review Investments

One of the biggest mistakes athletes make with money is checking it too often.

In baseball, no coach evaluates a player's season after every at-bat. Performance is measured over series, months, and full seasons. Constant evaluation leads to overreaction.

Investments work the same way.

Reviewing your portfolio too frequently invites emotion. Every up and down feels dramatic when you are staring at it daily. Long-term investing requires zooming out.

For most people, a structured review schedule works best:

- Quarterly check-ins for awareness
- Annual deep reviews for decisions
- Life-event reviews when circumstances change

In baseball terms, this is regular film study, not watching every pitch on replay.

The goal of reviewing is not to tinker. It is to confirm that your plan still fits your situation and that nothing has drifted too far off course.

If nothing needs to change, doing nothing is a win.

What Rebalancing Actually Means

Rebalancing is the process of bringing your portfolio back to its intended mix.

Over time, investments grow at different rates. Stocks may outperform bonds. One asset class may dominate others. Left alone, this changes your risk level without you realizing it.

Rebalancing restores balance.

For example:

- Stocks grow faster than expected
- Your portfolio becomes riskier than planned
- Rebalancing means trimming stocks and adding to bonds or cash

In baseball terms, this is lineup balance.

If your team suddenly has too many power hitters and no defense, you adjust. You do not bench your stars out of fear. You rebalance roles so the team still functions.

Rebalancing is not selling winners because they are bad.

It is selling winners because they grew larger than intended.

Common Rebalancing Strategies

There are a few practical ways to rebalance, and simplicity matters.

Time-based rebalancing

This means rebalancing on a set schedule, such as once per year. It removes emotion and keeps the process predictable.

Threshold-based rebalancing

This means rebalancing when an asset drifts beyond a certain percentage from its target. For example, if stocks move 5 percent above target, you rebalance.

Cash-flow rebalancing

This uses new contributions or withdrawals to restore balance instead of selling. You direct new money to underweight areas.

In baseball terms, this is adjusting roles using practice reps, lineup changes, and playing time rather than cutting players mid-season.

The best strategy is the one you will actually follow. Overcomplicated systems lead to mistakes.

Life Changes and Portfolio Updates

Some adjustments are not market-driven. They are life-driven.

Just like rosters change due to real-world factors, portfolios need updates when life changes.

Common triggers include:

- Job changes or income shifts
- Marriage or divorce
- Having children
- Buying a home
- Starting or selling a business
- Approaching retirement

- Health changes

These events change your risk capacity, time horizon, and cash needs.

In baseball terms, this is losing a starting pitcher or adding a key bat at the trade deadline. The game plan must adjust.

Ignoring life changes is like running the same lineup regardless of injuries. It eventually catches up to you.

Rebalancing after life events is not about maximizing returns. It is about protecting stability and flexibility.

Avoiding Over-Management

This is where many athletes get themselves in trouble.

They start with good intentions.

They read too much.

They check performance too often.

They make small changes constantly.

This is over-management.

In baseball terms, this is the coach who changes the lineup every game, pulls pitchers too early, and never lets players settle into roles. It creates tension, confusion, and poor performance.

Over-managed portfolios often:

- Chase recent performance
- Increase transaction costs
- Create tax consequences
- Increase stress
- Reduce long-term returns

Doing less is often doing more.

Rebalancing is not a reason to tinker with strategy, chase trends, or redesign your entire plan. It is a maintenance task, not a rebuild.

If your original plan was sound, the goal is to keep it intact, not reinvent it.

The Difference Between Adjustment and Reaction

This distinction matters.

Adjustments are intentional.

Reactions are emotional.

Adjustments are planned.

Reactions are rushed.

Adjustments follow rules.

Reactions follow feelings.

In baseball, great managers stick to strategy even when fans are yelling. They trust data, preparation, and long-term vision.

Financially, rebalancing is an adjustment. Panic selling is a reaction.

Knowing the difference keeps you from sabotaging yourself during volatility.

Coach's Perspective

A coach would keep it simple.

Stick to the plan.

Make smart adjustments.

Do not overcoach it.

Trust the process.

Next game.

Rebalancing is part of discipline. It is not a sign that something went wrong. It is proof that the system is working.

Game Situations and Decision Points

Your stocks have outperformed for several years. Do you let risk creep up or rebalance intentionally?

Markets are volatile. Do you make changes based on fear or stick to scheduled reviews?

Your income changes significantly. Do you update your plan or ignore the shift?

These are mid-season decisions. How you handle them determines the final standings.

Common Athlete Mistakes and Financial Parallels

Athletes overreact to short slumps.

Financially, that leads to unnecessary changes.

Athletes ignore fatigue and injuries.

Financially, that means ignoring life changes.

Athletes try to fix everything at once.

Financially, that leads to over-management.

Consistency beats chaos.

Winning the Long Game

Championship teams are not perfect. They are adaptable without being emotional.

Rebalancing allows you to:

- Control risk
- Stay aligned with goals
- Protect progress
- Avoid self-inflicted mistakes

You do not need to be constantly active to be effective. You need to be disciplined, aware, and patient.

That is how long seasons are won.

Athlete Takeaways

- Review your portfolio like film, not like live commentary.
- Rebalancing restores discipline, not doubt.
- Adjust for life changes the same way you adjust for injuries.
- Over-management creates more problems than it solves.
- Trust the plan, make smart mid-season moves, and finish strong.

Chapter 18: The Mental Game of Money

Every baseball player learns this lesson the hard way.

You can have perfect mechanics. You can be in great shape. You can prepare relentlessly. But when the mental side slips, performance follows. Slumps happen not because talent disappears, but because confidence wavers, frustration creeps in, and decision-making gets rushed.

Money has the same mental game.

Most financial mistakes are not caused by lack of intelligence. They are caused by emotions. Fear. Greed. Overconfidence. Pressure. Noise. The challenge is not knowing what to do. The challenge is doing it consistently when emotions are loud.

The mental game determines whether your financial plan survives real conditions.

Fear, Greed, and Overconfidence

These three emotions drive most poor financial decisions.

Fear shows up when markets fall, income changes, or uncertainty increases. Fear makes people freeze, sell at the wrong time, or avoid decisions entirely.

In baseball terms, fear is playing not to make a mistake. You stop swinging freely. You hesitate. You let good pitches go by. Eventually, you strike out looking.

Greed shows up when things are going well. Returns look strong. Stories circulate about easy money. Confidence turns into urgency. Greed pushes people to chase what is hot, abandon discipline, and take risks they do not fully understand.

In baseball terms, greed is trying to hit a five-run home run with the bases empty. You swing harder than necessary and lose balance.

Overconfidence shows up when early success convinces you that rules no longer apply. You made a good pick. You timed something right. Suddenly you believe skill outweighs process.

In baseball terms, this is believing one hot streak means you never need to watch film again.

None of these emotions are weaknesses. They are human. The mistake is letting them drive decisions.

Crowd Noise and Herd Behavior

Baseball players know how loud crowds can get.

Fans yell to swing. To bunt. To pull the pitcher. To bench the guy in a slump. Most of the noise is emotional, reactionary, and disconnected from long-term strategy.

Financial markets have even louder crowds.

Headlines. Social media. Friends. Podcasts. Influencers. Every day there is a new opinion, a new prediction, a new reason to panic or chase opportunity.

Herd behavior happens when people copy what others are doing because it feels safer than standing alone.

In baseball terms, this is chasing the league-wide trend instead of trusting your team identity. It might work for someone else. It may not fit you at all.

Following the crowd feels comfortable. It rarely produces disciplined results.

The market rewards patience. The crowd rewards excitement.

Why the Mental Game Is Harder Than the Math

The math of investing is simple.

The psychology is not.

You can understand:

- Diversification
- Compounding
- Long-term strategy
- Risk management

And still make bad decisions when emotions spike.

In baseball, players do not forget how to hit during slumps. They lose rhythm, confidence, and patience. The skill is still there, but execution suffers.

Financially, the same thing happens. Knowledge stays intact. Behavior breaks down.

That is why systems matter more than willpower.

Building Systems for Discipline

Great players do not rely on feel alone. They rely on routines.

Batting practice.

Pre-game preparation.

Film study.

Recovery protocols.

Systems remove decision-making from emotional moments.

Money needs the same structure.

Examples of financial systems include:

- Automatic savings and investing
- Pre-set asset allocation
- Scheduled portfolio reviews

- Clear rules for rebalancing
- Emergency funds that prevent panic
- Written financial plans

These systems do one thing well. They keep you from making decisions in the heat of the moment.

In baseball terms, this is trusting your approach at the plate even when you are 0-for-12. You do not reinvent your swing mid-game. You trust the work.

Discipline is easier when the system is already in place.

Staying Composed During Slumps

Every player slumps.

You feel late on fastballs.

Breaking balls look sharper.

Confidence dips.

Pressing begins.

Financial slumps feel similar.

Markets drop.

Accounts decline.

Plans feel shaky.

Doubt creeps in.

The worst thing you can do during a slump is abandon fundamentals.

In baseball, that leads to:

- Changing mechanics daily
- Over-swinging
- Forcing plays
- Losing trust in coaching

Financially, that leads to:

- Panic selling
- Chasing new strategies
- Over-managing portfolios
- Abandoning long-term plans

Slumps are part of the game. They are not signals to quit.

The athletes who last understand that composure is a competitive advantage.

The Role of Time and Perspective

Baseball teaches patience.

You cannot judge a hitter on one game.

You cannot judge a pitcher on one inning.

You cannot judge a season in April.

Money requires the same perspective.

Short-term results feel important because they are visible. Long-term results matter because they determine outcomes.

Zooming out reduces emotional intensity.

When fear or greed spikes, ask:

- Has my goal changed?
- Has my time horizon changed?
- Has my plan fundamentally broken?

If the answer is no, then emotion is the problem, not the strategy.

Coach's Perspective

A coach would say it without hesitation.

Control what you can control.

Next pitch.

Trust your preparation.

Do not let the crowd dictate your game.

Stay locked in.

Mental toughness is not ignoring emotion. It is managing it.

Financial success requires the same mental discipline as competitive sports.

Game Situations and Decision Points

Markets drop sharply. Do you review the plan or react to fear?

Everyone is talking about a hot investment. Do you chase it or stick to your system?

You have early success. Do you double down recklessly or stay disciplined?

These moments decide outcomes.

Just like baseball, the mental response matters more than the event itself.

Common Athlete Mistakes and Financial Parallels

Athletes press during slumps.

Financially, that leads to forced decisions.

Athletes listen too closely to crowd noise.

Financially, that leads to herd behavior.

Athletes confuse confidence with invincibility.

Financially, that leads to overconfidence and risk.

The same mental mistakes repeat across fields.

Winning the Long Game

Baseball seasons are long by design. They test patience, consistency, and mental toughness.

Financial lives are even longer.

You will experience:

- Ups and downs

- Hot streaks and slumps
- Confidence and doubt
- Calm and chaos

Winning does not require perfect timing or constant action. It requires staying composed, trusting your system, and stacking disciplined decisions over time.

The mental game is not optional. It is the game.

Athlete Takeaways

- Emotions drive mistakes when systems are missing.
- Fear and greed are signals, not instructions.
- Crowd noise is loud. Discipline is quiet.
- Slumps happen. Fundamentals survive them.
- Trust the process, stay composed, and keep taking good at-bats.

Part V: The Long Career and Life After Baseball

Every baseball player eventually reaches the same moment.

The season ends. The routine disappears. The uniform comes off.

Baseball gives you structure, identity, and daily purpose. When the game ends, that structure is gone overnight. Suddenly you are responsible for managing time, income, health, family, and long-term decisions without a coaching staff setting the schedule.

Your financial life enters a new season.

This part of the book is about thinking beyond one year or one contract. Financial success is not about winning a single inning. It is about managing decades.

From Seasons to a Lifetime

Baseball teaches patience over a season. Slumps happen. Hot streaks fade. What matters is consistency and adjustment over time.

Money works the same way, just longer.

Many former players make the mistake of treating money like a single at-bat. Big swings. Emotional decisions. Trying to make up ground quickly. That mindset creates pressure and mistakes.

The long career rewards discipline, not urgency.

Identity After the Game

When baseball ends, identity becomes a challenge. For years, being "the player" defined your role and value. When that disappears, some athletes chase feeling through spending, risk, or avoidance.

Financial discipline starts with knowing who you are without the uniform.

Your value is not tied to stats.

Your future is not defined by your last season.

This phase is about building something new with the same habits that made you successful in the game.

Your Career Is the New Franchise

After baseball, your career becomes your franchise.

Income replaces contracts.

Benefits replace facilities.

Reputation replaces stats.

Understanding money gives you leverage. It helps you make decisions from strength instead of fear and avoid panic when change shows up.

Protection, Family, and Stability

As life moves forward, priorities shift. Family, health, and responsibility matter more. Money becomes less about excitement and more about protection and flexibility.

Strong teams plan ahead. Strong financial lives do too.

Coach's Perspective

Finish strong.

Think long-term.

Prepare for what's next.

Handle your business.

The best careers are not the flashiest. They are the most durable.

Chapter 19: Taxes and Where You Play Your Money

Every baseball player learns this early.

Where you play matters.

A hitter's numbers change depending on the ballpark. Some parks favor power. Others suppress offense. The same swing can be a home run in one stadium and a routine fly ball in another. Smart teams understand this. They do not evaluate performance without context.

Taxes work the same way with money.

It is not just about *what* you earn or *how* you invest. It is about **where** your money plays. The same investment can produce very different results depending on the account it sits in. Ignoring taxes is like ignoring ballpark dimensions. You might still compete, but you leave runs on the table.

This chapter is about learning the field.

Taxable vs Tax-Advantaged Accounts

At the highest level, money lives in two places.

Taxable accounts

These include checking accounts, savings accounts, brokerage accounts, and anything not wrapped in special tax rules. When you earn interest, dividends, or capital gains, taxes show up. Every year. No delay.

Tax-advantaged accounts

These include retirement accounts and other vehicles that receive special treatment under tax law. Examples include 401(k)s, IRAs, and similar plans. Taxes are either delayed or eliminated depending on the structure.

In baseball terms, taxable accounts are like playing in a neutral park. Nothing special helps or hurts you. Tax-advantaged accounts are like hitter-friendly parks or pitcher-friendly parks. Same skills. Better conditions.

Taxes are one of the biggest drags on long-term results. Using the right accounts is how you reduce that drag legally and intentionally.

Tax-Deferred vs Tax-Free Growth

Not all tax-advantaged accounts work the same way.

Tax-deferred growth

With tax-deferred accounts, you get a tax break now. Money goes in before taxes. It grows without being taxed each year. You pay taxes later when you take it out.

This is like deferring fatigue. You push harder now, knowing you will deal with it later.

Examples include traditional 401(k)s and traditional IRAs.

Tax-free growth

With tax-free accounts, you pay taxes upfront. Once the money is inside, qualified growth and withdrawals are tax-free.

This is like front-loading the work so the late innings are easier.

Examples include Roth IRAs and Roth 401(k)s.

Neither is automatically better. The right choice depends on income level, career stage, and future expectations. The mistake is not choosing at all.

Asset Location Basics

Asset allocation is what you own.

Asset location is where you hold it.

This distinction matters.

Some investments create more taxes than others. Interest income, short-term gains, and high-turnover strategies generate more tax friction. Long-term growth assets tend to be more tax-efficient.

In baseball terms, this is lineup construction. You do not bat everyone the same way in every situation. You put players where they succeed.

General principles athletes should understand:

- Tax-inefficient investments often belong in tax-advantaged accounts
- Tax-efficient investments often work better in taxable accounts
- Location decisions compound over time, just like returns

You do not need to master tax law. You need to respect that placement matters.

Why Athletes Miss This

Athletes often focus on performance, not structure.

They chase returns, not efficiency. They talk about investments without discussing where those investments live. That is like scouting hitters without checking where they play half their games.

Money myths sound like this:

- "A good investment is good everywhere"
- "Taxes only matter later"
- "I'll deal with that when I'm older"

Those beliefs cost real money over long careers.

Taxes show up quietly. They do not feel dramatic. But they compound against you if ignored.

Common Tax Mistakes Players Make

Most mistakes are not complicated. They are avoidable.

- Using only taxable accounts when tax-advantaged options are available

- Ignoring employer retirement plans
- Mixing investments randomly without regard to tax impact
- Triggering unnecessary short-term gains
- Failing to plan withdrawals

In baseball terms, these are unforced errors. Missed cutoffs. Bad base running. Mental mistakes that do not show up as highlight plays but change outcomes.

Coach's Perspective

A coach would say it clearly.

Know the field.

Play the conditions.

Do not beat yourself.

Win the small battles.

Taxes are part of the game. Pretending otherwise does not make you aggressive. It makes you careless.

Game Situations and Decision Points

You have two accounts available.

Do you put the same investment in both, or choose intentionally?

You earn more income.

Do you adjust where you save, or keep doing what you have always done?

You hear about a great investment.

Do you ask how it is taxed, or just how it performed?

Context matters.

Winning the Long Game

You cannot eliminate taxes.

You can manage them.

Over a long financial career, smart placement can be the difference between staying ahead and constantly playing catch-up. The goal is not perfection. It is awareness and discipline.

Great teams know their park.

Great financial plans know their accounts.

Athlete Takeaways

- Where your money plays matters
- Tax-deferred and tax-free growth are different tools
- Asset location is about efficiency, not excitement
- Most tax mistakes are unforced errors
- Smart players respect the field and play accordingly

Chapter 20: Retirement Accounts and Financial Independence

Every baseball player understands the value of the farm system. Championship teams are not built only through big free-agent signings. They are built by developing talent over time, investing early, and trusting the process long before the results show up on the scoreboard.

Retirement accounts work the same way.

They are not exciting. They do not provide instant gratification. They exist to create independence later by doing the quiet work now. Most athletes understand development in sports. The challenge is learning to respect development in money.

This chapter is about building your financial farm system so you are not forced to scramble in the later innings of life.

401(k)s and Employer Plans

Employer-sponsored retirement plans are often the first real investing opportunity athletes encounter outside of sports.

A 401(k) allows you to invest part of your paycheck before it ever hits your bank account. That automatic structure matters. When money never touches your checking account, you are less tempted to spend it.

In baseball terms, this is automatic reps. You do not debate whether to show up. You are already there.

Many employer plans include a match. This is free money tied to your contribution. Ignoring a match is like leaving runners on base. You may still score later, but you missed an easy opportunity.

Key things to understand about employer plans:

- Contributions often come directly from payroll
- Matches reward consistency, not timing
- Investment choices may be limited but functional
- Discipline matters more than perfection

Athletes sometimes delay participation because they want more control. That delay costs time, and time is the most valuable asset in retirement planning.

Traditional vs Roth IRAs

IRAs give you flexibility outside of employer plans.

A **Traditional IRA** allows tax-deferred growth. You may receive a tax deduction today. The money grows without annual taxes, but withdrawals are taxed later.

A **Roth IRA** works in reverse. You pay taxes now, but future qualified withdrawals are tax-free.

In baseball terms, this is choosing when to absorb fatigue. Do you push harder early or later? Both approaches can work depending on the season.

Early-career athletes often benefit from Roth contributions because income may be lower and time is long. Later-career athletes may benefit from tax deferral when income is higher.

The mistake is thinking one option is always better. The right choice depends on your current situation and future expectations.

Contribution Rules and Limits

Retirement accounts reward consistency, not aggression.

There are limits on how much you can contribute each year. These limits change over time, but the principle stays the same. Small, repeated contributions beat sporadic big swings.

In baseball terms, this is getting on base every game. You do not need a home run every at-bat. You need steady production.

Important concepts athletes should understand:

- Contribution limits are annual
- Missing years cannot be fully made up later
- Catch-up contributions exist later in life
- Consistency compounds faster than intensity

Waiting until you feel ready often means starting late. Starting small but early builds confidence and momentum.

Withdrawal Rules and Access

Retirement accounts are designed for the long game.

Accessing money early often comes with penalties and taxes. These rules exist to protect you from short-term decisions that hurt long-term independence.

In baseball terms, this is the difference between using a reliever correctly and burning them too early. You might solve today's problem but lose tomorrow's game.

Understanding withdrawal rules matters because:

- Early withdrawals can trigger penalties
- Taxes can erase years of growth
- Emergency planning should happen outside retirement accounts

Retirement money should not be your emergency fund. It should be protected so it can do its job uninterrupted.

What Financial Independence Really Means

Retirement is not about an age.

It is about control.

Financial independence means your basic needs can be met without relying on a paycheck. It does not require luxury. It requires consistency, planning, and patience.

In baseball terms, this is playing with a lead. You can be selective. You can rest when needed. You are not forcing plays out of desperation.

Retirement income often comes from multiple sources:

- Employer plans
- IRAs
- Taxable investments
- Social Security or pensions
- Part-time or passion work

The goal is flexibility, not a single number.

Why Athletes Struggle With Retirement Planning

Athletes are trained for the present.

Seasons are short. Careers are uncertain. The instinct is to focus on now. That mindset wins games. Financially, it can delay preparation.

Common thoughts sound like this:

- Retirement is too far away
- I will deal with it later
- I need the money now
- I will catch up

The reality is that catching up is harder than staying consistent. Time compounds whether you participate or not.

Coach's Perspective

A coach would not sugarcoat this.

Stack good days.

Reps matter.

Do not cheat the work.

Prepare for the long season.

Retirement planning is boring for the same reason conditioning is boring. It works.

Game Situations and Decision Points

Your employer offers a match.

Do you contribute or pass?

You have extra cash.

Do you upgrade lifestyle or fund future freedom?

You want access to money.

Do you pull from retirement or build separate savings?

These decisions feel small. Over decades, they decide outcomes.

Winning the Long Game

You do not retire from discipline.

You retire from obligation.

Retirement accounts are not about stopping work. They are about choosing how you spend your time when competition ends. The earlier you respect that, the more control you have later.

Championship organizations plan years ahead.

Strong financial lives do too.

Athlete Takeaways

- Retirement accounts are long-term farm systems
- Employer matches are free runs. Do not leave them stranded
- Traditional and Roth accounts serve different seasons
- Consistency beats late catch-up efforts
- Financial independence is about control, not age

Chapter 21: Housing and Big Financial Decisions

Every baseball player remembers the first time they signed a long-term contract or watched a teammate do it.

The excitement is real. So is the responsibility. Once you commit, flexibility changes. You gain stability, but you also give something up. That tradeoff is not good or bad. It is situational.

Housing and other big financial decisions work the same way.

They are not trophies. They are commitments. When made at the right time, they support your life and career. When made too early or for the wrong reasons, they quietly limit your options.

This chapter is about learning when to commit, when to stay flexible, and how to avoid letting ego or pressure make expensive decisions for you.

Renting vs Buying

There is no more emotional financial decision than housing.

Buying is often framed as winning. Renting is often framed as losing. That framing is wrong.

Renting provides flexibility.

Buying provides stability and long-term potential.

In baseball terms, renting is like a one-year deal. You can relocate. You can adjust quickly if circumstances change. You are not responsible for long-term maintenance, repairs, or market swings.

Buying is like signing a multi-year contract. You gain equity and control, but you commit to location, expenses, and responsibility.

Neither option is superior on its own. The right choice depends on timing, not pride.

Questions athletes should ask before buying:

- Is my income stable and predictable?
- Do I expect to stay in this location for several years?
- Can I handle maintenance and unexpected costs?
- Do I want flexibility right now or certainty?

Buying too early is like committing to a lineup spot before earning it. You might survive, but mistakes cost more.

The Hidden Costs of Homeownership

Many athletes focus only on the purchase price.

Ownership includes far more than the mortgage.

Property taxes.

Insurance.

Maintenance.

Repairs.

HOA fees.

Utilities.

Time and stress.

In baseball terms, this is playing without depth. Everything looks fine until one injury or slump hits, and suddenly the margin for error is gone.

Homeownership can be a powerful wealth-building tool when it fits your life. It becomes a burden when it does not.

Owning does not automatically mean building wealth. Buying the wrong property at the wrong time can slow progress for years.

Mortgages and Down Payments

A mortgage is leverage.

It allows you to control a large asset with a relatively small amount of money upfront. Leverage can help you build wealth. It can also magnify mistakes.

In baseball terms, this is swinging for extra bases. It can pay off, but only if timing and execution are right.

Down payments matter because they determine:

- Monthly payment size
- Interest paid over time
- Financial flexibility
- Risk if values decline

Smaller down payments increase leverage and risk. Larger down payments reduce risk but tie up cash.

There is no universal correct answer. The right down payment balances protection and flexibility.

Athletes often underestimate how valuable liquidity is early in a career. Cash gives you options. Options reduce stress. Stress leads to poor decisions.

Cars, Leases, and Financing Traps

Few purchases drain athletes faster than vehicles.

Cars feel harmless because payments are spread out. The damage shows up slowly, then all at once.

In baseball terms, this is committing errors that do not show up in the box score until the end of the game.

Common traps include:

- Buying more car than income supports
- Rolling negative equity into new loans

- Leasing without understanding total cost
- Financing luxury vehicles early in a career

Cars are depreciating assets. They lose value over time. That does not mean you cannot enjoy a nice car. It means you should understand what it costs you in future options.

A reliable, paid-off car provides flexibility. A high payment limits choices long after the excitement fades.

Lifestyle Pressure and Identity

Athletes face unique pressure around appearance.

Teammates notice. Friends notice. Social media notices. It can feel like success needs to look a certain way.

That pressure leads to decisions that are about image, not fit.

In baseball terms, this is pressing at the plate because you want to prove something. The swing gets bigger. Timing gets worse. Results suffer.

Your housing and vehicle choices should support your life, not validate it.

Real success shows up later, when pressure hits and you still have options.

Planning Major Purchases

Big purchases should never be emotional.

That includes homes, vehicles, businesses, and large lifestyle upgrades.

Before committing, ask:

- How does this affect monthly cash flow?
- What happens if income drops?
- Does this limit future flexibility?
- Am I buying this for function or for validation?

In baseball terms, this is knowing the count and situation. Sometimes the right move is to swing. Sometimes the right move is to take the pitch.

Patience is a skill. So is restraint.

Coach's Perspective

A coach would say it clearly.

Know the situation.

Do not put yourself in a bad count.

Protect flexibility.

Make decisions you can live with in the late innings.

Big commitments require big awareness.

Game Situations and Decision Points

You feel pressure to buy because everyone else is.

Do you evaluate timing or follow the crowd?

You qualify for a larger loan.

Do you ask what you can afford or what you should take?

You want an upgrade.

Do you check the long-term impact or focus on today?

Same game. Same rules.

Common Athlete Mistakes and Financial Parallels

Athletes rush commitments.

Financially, that means buying too early.

Athletes confuse confidence with readiness.

Financially, that leads to over-leverage.

Athletes chase image.

Financially, that creates long-term pressure.

The mistakes look different, but the pattern is the same.

Winning the Long Game

Housing and big purchases are not milestones to check off. They are strategic decisions that shape your future.

The goal is not to look successful today.

The goal is to stay flexible tomorrow.

Great careers are built by players who understand timing. Great financial lives are built the same way.

Athlete Takeaways

- Renting and buying are tools, not trophies
- Mortgages and leverage magnify both gains and mistakes
- Cars should support your life, not define it
- Big purchases deserve situational awareness
- Protect flexibility and play for the late innings

Chapter 22: Your Career Is Your Franchise

Every baseball organization knows this truth:

Players come and go, but the franchise is built to last.

Stadiums change. Rosters turn over. Front offices adjust strategy. What survives is the system that develops talent, manages risk, and plans beyond the next season.

Your career works the same way.

Your job is not just a paycheck. It is the engine that funds everything else in your financial life. Your savings. Your investments. Your lifestyle. Your future flexibility. If you neglect the franchise, no amount of smart investing can fully compensate.

This chapter is about treating your career with the same intentionality teams use to build winning organizations.

Salary vs Total Compensation

Most athletes focus on one number: salary.

That makes sense. It is visible. It is easy to compare. It feels like success.

But salary is only part of the picture.

Total compensation includes:

- Base pay
- Bonuses and incentives

- Health insurance
- Retirement plan contributions and matching
- Paid time off
- Flexibility and schedule control
- Growth and advancement opportunities

In baseball terms, salary is batting average. Total compensation is on-base percentage, slugging, defense, durability, and clubhouse role combined.

A higher salary with poor benefits can leave you worse off than a slightly lower salary with strong support. Health coverage alone can swing outcomes dramatically. Employer retirement matches are free money. Flexibility can protect mental and physical health.

Smart players evaluate the full stat line, not just one column.

Job Changes and Benefits

Changing teams can be powerful. It can also be disruptive.

A new job may increase pay, improve lifestyle, or open doors. It can also reset benefits, restart vesting schedules, and introduce risk if the role is not what it seemed.

In baseball terms, this is free agency. Sometimes it works perfectly. Sometimes the fit is wrong, and production drops.

Before making a move, ask:

- What benefits do I gain or lose?
- Does retirement matching reset?
- How stable is this role or organization?
- Am I moving toward growth or just reacting to frustration?

Job changes should be strategic, not emotional. Momentum matters. Stability matters. Short-term pay bumps can hide long-term setbacks.

Negotiation Basics

Negotiation makes many people uncomfortable.

That discomfort costs money over time.

Negotiation is not confrontation. It is communication. It is clarity. It is understanding your value and asking questions before accepting terms.

In baseball terms, this is contract negotiation. You do not apologize for advocating for yourself. You prepare. You understand the market. You protect your future.

Key principles:

- Know your value before you talk
- Ask questions instead of making demands
- Understand the full compensation package
- Be professional, not emotional

You are not being difficult. You are being responsible. Silence does not earn leverage. Preparation does.

Side Income and Entrepreneurship

Side income can be a powerful tool.

It can increase flexibility, accelerate savings, and reduce reliance on a single employer. It can also add complexity, time pressure, and risk.

In baseball terms, this is adding a secondary position. It can extend your career if managed well. It can hurt performance if it distracts from your primary role.

Side income should:

- Support long-term goals
- Fit your time and energy capacity
- Not jeopardize your primary income
- Be intentional, not impulsive

Not every opportunity is worth taking. Just because you can do something does not mean you should do it right now.

Entrepreneurship rewards patience, planning, and discipline. It punishes shortcuts and overconfidence.

Career Risk Is Financial Risk

Your career stability affects every financial decision.

Income volatility changes how much risk you can take with investments. Benefits affect how much you need to self-insure. Growth opportunities shape long-term earning potential.

Ignoring your career while obsessing over investments is like focusing on batting gloves while neglecting swing mechanics.

The franchise comes first.

Coach's Perspective

A coach would frame it simply.

Know your role.

Prepare for the long season.

Protect your body and availability.

Think beyond today.

Careers are built with consistency, not just talent.

Game Situations and Decision Points

You receive a job offer.

Do you evaluate total compensation or just salary?

You feel underpaid.

Do you prepare for negotiation or avoid the conversation?

A side opportunity appears.

Do you assess fit or chase excitement?

Career decisions compound just like financial ones.

Common Athlete Mistakes and Financial Parallels

Athletes chase short-term stats.

Financially, that means chasing salary alone.

Athletes ignore recovery.

Financially, that means burnout and instability.

Athletes overload themselves.

Financially, that leads to scattered focus.

The same discipline that builds careers builds financial strength.

Winning the Long Game

Your career is your franchise.

Treat it with intention. Protect it. Develop it. Do not let frustration or comparison drive decisions that shape decades of outcomes.

Strong financial lives are built on strong earning engines. Investing matters, but it comes second to sustainable income and thoughtful career management.

Athlete Takeaways

- Salary is only one stat; total compensation tells the real story
- Job changes should be strategic, not emotional
- Negotiation is preparation, not confrontation
- Side income should support, not distract
- Protect the franchise and everything else gets easier

Chapter 24: Talking About Money With Family

Every baseball team depends on communication.

Signs from the dugout. Conversations between innings. Quiet reminders from veterans to rookies. When communication breaks down, mistakes multiply. Missed signs lead to outs. Confusion creates tension. Small issues turn into big innings.

Money works the same way in families.

Most money problems are not really about money. They are about expectations, fear, pride, responsibility, and silence. Families avoid these conversations because they feel uncomfortable, emotional, or risky. But avoiding them does not protect relationships. It strains them.

Talking about money is not about control. It is about clarity.

Why Money Conversations Are So Hard

Money carries emotion.

It represents security.

It represents success or failure.

It represents sacrifice and opportunity.

In baseball terms, money conversations are like mound visits in a tight game. Nobody wants to call time, but when something is off, ignoring it only makes the next pitch worse.

Silence creates assumptions.

Assumptions create resentment.

Resentment damages trust.

Clear conversations prevent all three.

Teaching Kids About Money

Kids learn money habits long before they understand money concepts.

They watch:

- How you spend
- How you save
- How you react to stress
- How you talk about money

What you model matters more than what you say.

In baseball terms, this is fundamentals. You do not just explain how to field a ground ball. You show it. Over and over.

Teaching kids about money does not require complex lessons. It requires consistency.

Simple ideas go a long way:

- Money is finite
- Choices have trade-offs
- Saving creates options
- Patience matters

Allowance, chores, saving for goals, and delayed gratification all build confidence. The goal is not perfection. The goal is comfort and awareness.

Kids who grow up seeing money discussed calmly are far less likely to fear it later.

College and Young Adults

This is a critical transition point.

College and early adulthood often bring:

- Credit cards
- Student loans
- First real paychecks
- Independent decisions

Many young adults feel pressure to appear successful before they are stable. That pressure leads to mistakes.

In baseball terms, this is a call-up to the big leagues. The lights are brighter. The speed is faster. The margin for error is smaller.

Families can help by:

- Talking openly about budgeting and debt
- Setting expectations around support
- Explaining trade-offs instead of issuing rules

Support without structure creates dependency. Structure without support creates resentment. Balance matters.

The goal is not to control decisions. It is to help young adults understand consequences before they learn the hard way.

Aging Parents and Caregiving

As careers progress, roles often reverse.

Parents age. Health changes. Financial complexity increases. Caregiving becomes part of life.

These transitions are emotionally heavy and financially complex. Avoiding conversations early makes later decisions harder.

In baseball terms, this is a veteran passing leadership responsibilities.

Timing matters.

Important conversations include:

- Who manages finances if needed
- Where important documents are located
- Healthcare wishes
- Living arrangements and support expectations

These conversations should happen before crisis hits. Waiting until the ninth inning with the bases loaded is not a strategy.

Clarity early reduces stress later.

Family Expectations and Boundaries

Helping family financially without clarity often creates problems.

Unspoken expectations lead to:

- Resentment
- Guilt
- Dependency
- Conflict

Boundaries protect relationships.

In baseball terms, boundaries are defensive assignments. If no one knows their role, collisions happen.

Before helping family financially, be clear:

- What you can do
- What you cannot do
- Whether support is temporary or ongoing
- Whether expectations exist

Support should be intentional, not reactive. Saying yes without clarity often causes more damage than saying no with honesty.

Navigating Difficult Conversations

Money conversations feel heavy because stakes feel personal.

Approach them with:

- Curiosity instead of judgment
- Listening instead of lecturing
- Honesty instead of avoidance

You do not need perfect words. You need respect and clarity.

In baseball terms, this is in-game communication. Calm voices keep teams steady. Emotional reactions create errors.

Silence is not neutral. It is a decision with consequences.

Coach's Perspective

A coach would emphasize communication.

Talk early.

Be clear.

Respect roles.

Protect the team.

Teams that communicate survive pressure. Families do too.

Game Situations and Decision Points

A family member asks for help.

Do you pause and clarify or react emotionally?

A child asks about money.

Do you engage or avoid?

Tension builds around finances.

Do you address it or hope it passes?

Just like baseball, ignoring signs leads to mistakes.

Common Athlete Mistakes and Financial Parallels

Athletes avoid tough conversations.

Financially, that leads to misunderstandings.

Athletes overextend themselves.

Financially, that leads to resentment.

Athletes assume alignment.

Financially, that leads to conflict.

Clear communication prevents all three.

Winning the Long Game

Healthy money conversations strengthen families.

When expectations are clear and communication is respectful, money becomes a tool instead of a wedge. Relationships improve. Stress decreases. Trust grows.

That is long-term success.

Athlete Takeaways

- Money conversations are about clarity, not control
- Kids learn money habits through observation
- Young adults need structure, not silence
- Boundaries protect relationships
- Honest communication keeps the family team together

Part VI: Staying in the Game

Every baseball season tests more than talent.

Long road trips. Slumps. Injuries. Bad calls. Fatigue. The teams that last are not the ones with the most highlights. They are the ones that stay composed, adjust when needed, and keep showing up every day. Talent matters, but durability matters more.

Your financial life works the same way.

Staying in the game is not about one good decision or one big win. It is about consistency over time. It is about avoiding mistakes that knock you out early and building systems that keep you moving forward even when conditions are not perfect.

This final section focuses on sustainability.

Financial success is rarely about being right all the time. It is about being disciplined enough to avoid self-inflicted wounds. Scams, bad advice, emotional decisions, and shortcuts do more damage than market downturns ever will. Awareness is your defense.

Just like baseball, money rewards players who respect the grind. You will have hot streaks and cold streaks. You will feel confident at times and uncertain at others. What matters is that you stay within your system and do not abandon fundamentals when pressure shows up.

Strong players know when to ask for help. They listen to coaches. They trust preparation. Financially, that means knowing when to seek professional guidance, recognizing red flags, and avoiding promises that sound too good to be true. There are no guarantees in baseball, and there are no guarantees in money.

Staying in the game also means thinking long-term. Careers change. Income changes. Life changes. The goal is not perfection. The goal is resilience. You want a financial plan that can absorb setbacks without falling apart.

Baseball teaches patience. One at-bat does not define a season. One mistake does not define a career. Financial progress works the same way. Stack good days. Make small, smart decisions consistently. Let time do its work.

If you do that, you give yourself the best chance to stay on the field long after the final out.

Chapter 25: Advisors, Scams, and Playing the Long Game

Every baseball player eventually learns this truth.

You cannot do everything yourself.

You may be talented. You may outwork most people. You may study film, lift consistently, and take pride in your preparation. But even the best players do not develop in isolation. Coaches see what you cannot see. Trainers catch small issues before they become season-ending injuries. Veteran teammates help you avoid mistakes they already paid for.

Money works the same way.

The athletes who succeed financially over decades are not the ones who try to prove they can do everything alone. They are the ones who know when to get help, how to evaluate advice, and how to ignore noise that does not serve them.

This chapter is about staying in the game.

When to Seek Professional Help

There is a common misconception that financial advisors are only for the ultra-wealthy or for people who have already made big mistakes. That belief keeps athletes from getting help when it would matter most.

In reality, professional help is most valuable during transitions.

You should seriously consider outside guidance when:

- Your income increases or becomes unpredictable
- You receive a signing bonus, NIL income, inheritance, or business payout
- You change jobs or careers
- You get married or start a family
- You buy or sell a home or business
- Taxes start to feel confusing or stressful
- You feel unsure but keep delaying decisions

In baseball terms, this is moving up a level.

The pitching is faster. The scouting is better. The margin for error shrinks. At higher levels, support increases. It does not disappear.

Waiting until something breaks is like waiting until your elbow blows out before talking to a trainer. Preparation comes first.

Seeking help is not a sign that you cannot handle things. It is a sign that you take responsibility seriously.

Types of Financial Advisors

Not all advisors serve the same role, and misunderstanding this is where many athletes get burned.

There are three broad categories you will encounter most often:

Fee-only advisors

These advisors are paid directly by the client for advice. They do not earn commissions for selling products. Their compensation is transparent, and their role is usually focused on planning and guidance.

Fee-based advisors

These advisors may charge fees and also earn commissions depending on the services or products used. This does not automatically make them bad, but it requires more questions and clarity.

Commission-based advisors

These advisors earn money primarily by selling financial products. Their income depends on transactions. That creates incentives that may or may not align with your needs.

In baseball terms, this is role clarity.

You would not ask a pitching coach to redesign your swing. You would not ask a strength coach to call pitches. Each role exists for a reason. Financial advice is no different.

Before working with anyone, ask:

- How are you paid?
- What services do you provide?
- Who is your typical client?
- How do you help people in situations like mine?
- Are you required to act in my best interest?

If someone cannot answer clearly, that is information.

Recognizing Scams and Bad Advice

Athletes are targeted more than they realize.

Income often arrives before education. Confidence is high. Time feels abundant. That combination attracts bad actors.

Scams and bad advice usually share common traits:

- Promises of guaranteed returns
- Pressure to act quickly
- "Exclusive" or insider opportunities
- Vague explanations
- Complexity that cannot be clearly explained
- Advice that ignores your full financial picture

Bad advice often sounds confident and urgent. It appeals to ego and fear at the same time.

In baseball terms, this is being rushed into a bunt sign with no preparation, no communication, and no understanding of the situation. It might work once. Long-term, it creates outs.

If someone discourages you from asking questions, slowing down, or getting a second opinion, that is a red flag.

Trust is earned through transparency, not pressure.

Ten Common Financial Mistakes Athletes Make

Most financial damage does not come from lack of intelligence. It comes from behavior under pressure.

Here are ten mistakes that show up again and again:

1. Avoiding planning because it feels overwhelming
2. Letting lifestyle rise with income automatically
3. Ignoring taxes until filing time
4. Carrying high-interest debt too long
5. Chasing hype instead of fundamentals
6. Letting emotion drive investment decisions
7. Skipping retirement contributions early
8. Failing to adjust plans as life changes
9. Avoiding hard conversations with family or partners
10. Waiting too long to start or correct habits

None of these mistakes happen overnight. They compound quietly.

Just like baseball, it is rarely one bad play that loses the season. It is repeated mental errors.

Ten Rules for Long-Term Financial Success

Long-term success is built the same way championships are built. Simple rules. Executed consistently.

1. Live below your means, regardless of income
2. Automate saving and investing
3. Protect what you build with insurance and planning

4. Stay diversified
5. Keep costs and fees low
6. Be patient during slumps and streaks
7. Adjust intentionally, not emotionally
8. Ask for help before problems escalate
9. Ignore noise, trends, and comparison
10. Stay consistent even when progress feels slow

These rules are not exciting. They are effective.

Most people fail not because they do not know these rules, but because they abandon them when pressure hits.

Coach's Perspective

A coach would not complicate this.

They would say it directly.

Get the right help.

Do not chase shortcuts.

Trust preparation.

Do not beat yourself.

Finish strong.

Coaches understand something athletes sometimes forget after the uniform comes off.

Nobody wins alone.

Game Situations and Decision Points

Consider these moments.

You receive a large paycheck or bonus.

Do you build a plan, or do you assume momentum will carry you?

You hear about a "can't miss" opportunity.

Do you slow down and evaluate, or do you rush because you feel behind?

You realize you are stressed about money but avoid asking for help.

Do you keep guessing, or do you bring in support?

These are not money problems. They are decision problems.

The same awareness that wins close games wins financially.

Common Athlete Mistakes and Financial Parallels

Athletes rely on confidence alone.

Financially, that leads to ignoring risk.

Athletes chase momentum.

Financially, that leads to poor timing.

Athletes resist coaching.

Financially, that leads to repeated mistakes.

Discipline off the field matters just as much as discipline on it.

Winning the Long Game

Baseball careers are finite.

Financial lives are not.

The goal is not perfection. The goal is durability. Staying available. Avoiding mistakes that take you out of the game entirely.

With the right advisors, clear rules, and consistent habits, money becomes a tool instead of a source of stress. Progress compounds. Confidence grows.

You do not need to swing for the fences to win.

You need to stay in the lineup.

Athlete Takeaways

- Get help when the game speeds up
- Know who you are listening to and how they are paid
- Guaranteed returns and urgency are red flags
- Most financial damage comes from behavior, not markets
- Fundamentals, discipline, and patience win the long game

Chapter 26: Losing the Schedule and Rebuilding Structure

Every baseball player remembers the first offseason without a team-issued schedule.

No mandatory lifts.

No early bus.

No practice times on the whiteboard.

No coach checking attendance.

At first, it feels like freedom. Sleep in. Train when you want. Decide your own pace. But over time, something shifts. Workouts get pushed back. Film study disappears. Conditioning becomes optional. What once felt like flexibility quietly turns into drift.

Life after baseball works the same way, especially with money.

When someone else sets your calendar, structure is automatic. When no one does, discipline becomes optional. And optional discipline is where habits start to break.

Why Life Gets Harder When No One Is Setting Your Calendar

In baseball, structure is everywhere.

Practice times are fixed.

Lifts are scheduled.

Travel is planned.

Games start when they start.

You do not have to decide when to train. You just show up and execute.

After the game, that framework disappears.

No one tells you when to wake up.

No one tells you when to train.

No one tells you when to check your finances.

No one tells you when to plan for the future.

This is where many former players struggle, not because they lack discipline, but because discipline without structure is much harder than discipline inside structure.

Money suffers first.

Bills still come, but no one reminds you.

Saving is important, but no one enforces it.

Planning matters, but nothing breaks immediately if you skip it.

Baseball punished missed reps quickly. Money punishes missed structure slowly. That delay is dangerous.

From Mandatory Workouts to Optional Discipline

Mandatory workouts remove negotiation.

You do not debate whether to lift. You lift because it is on the schedule.

You do not decide if conditioning matters. It is already planned.

Once workouts become optional, the mind gets involved. And the mind is excellent at negotiating.

"I'll do it tomorrow."

"I'll catch up later."

"I've earned a break."

Financial discipline becomes optional the same way.

Saving turns into "if there's anything left."

Budgeting turns into "I have a general idea."

Reviewing accounts turns into "I'll look later."

Nothing explodes right away. That is why it feels safe. But just like skipping conditioning, the cost shows up later when you are tired, behind, and scrambling.

Optional discipline always loses to convenience.

How Lack of Structure Quietly Breaks Financial Habits

Most financial problems do not come from one big mistake. They come from a thousand small skips.

Skipping savings one month.

Ignoring statements.

Letting subscriptions pile up.

Paying minimums without a plan.

Without structure, habits erode quietly.

In baseball, skipping reps shows up in timing.

In money, skipping structure shows up in stress.

You feel behind but cannot explain why.

You earn money but never feel comfortable.

You avoid looking because it feels overwhelming.

This is the financial version of losing your routine. You are still talented. You still work hard. But without structure, performance drops.

Replacing Practice Schedules With Personal Systems

When teams trust veterans, they often remove guardrails. The expectation is simple. You know what to do. Now do it yourself.

The players who last are the ones who rebuild structure intentionally.

Money requires the same shift.

You must replace external structure with personal systems.

A system does not rely on motivation.

A system runs even when you are busy.

A system works even when you are tired.

Examples of financial systems include:

Automatic savings transfers

Scheduled bill pay

Monthly financial check-ins

Simple budgets you actually use

Clear rules for spending and saving

This is the financial equivalent of creating your own offseason plan. Same reps. Same consistency. New accountability.

Building a Personal Calendar for Money

Baseball success is calendar-based.

Lift days.

Bullpen days.

Rest days.

Game days.

Money needs the same rhythm.

Pick a day each month to review accounts.

Pick a day each quarter to revisit goals.

Pick a system that runs without constant decision-making.

When money decisions live on the calendar, they stop living in your head. Stress drops. Confidence rises.

Structure reduces noise.

Coach's Perspective

A coach would not sugarcoat this.

Nobody is coming to save you.

No one is setting the schedule anymore.

That does not mean standards drop.

What would a coach say?

"Be a pro."

"Handle your business."

"Do not cheat the work."

"Reps matter even when no one is watching."

"How you practice is how you play."

Financial success is not about intensity. It is about consistency when no one is forcing you.

Game Situations and Decision Points

You get paid with no plan.

Do you react, or follow your system?

Your schedule gets busy.

Do you skip reviewing finances, or protect the routine?

You feel fine financially.

Do you assume that means things are working, or verify it?

These are everyday decisions. Over a season, they define outcomes.

Common Athlete Mistakes and Financial Parallels

Athletes rely on structure too long.

Financially, that shows up as no system after sports.

Athletes confuse freedom with rest.

Financially, that leads to drift.

Athletes skip boring reps.

Financially, that creates instability.

Baseball careers end quickly. Financial habits last decades.

Winning the Long Game

The players who succeed after baseball are not the ones who stay the most intense. They are the ones who stay the most structured.

They rebuild routines.

They replace team schedules with personal systems.

They understand that discipline without structure fades fast.

Money rewards the same approach.

Structure creates calm.

Calm creates clarity.

Clarity creates good decisions.

You do not need perfection. You need consistency you can maintain.

Athlete Takeaways

- No schedule means no excuses. Build your own structure.
- Optional discipline always loses. Systems win.
- Small skipped reps create big problems over time.
- Put money on a calendar the same way you put training on one.
- Professionals create structure even when no one is watching.

Chapter 27: From Teammates to Coworkers

Every baseball player remembers their first day in a new clubhouse.

You did not know the hierarchy yet.

You did not know who led vocally and who led quietly.

You did not know what mistakes were tolerated and which ones got you benched.

So you watched. You listened. You learned the culture.

Leaving baseball and entering the traditional workplace feels like that moment multiplied, except this time there is no clubhouse guide, no veteran pulling you aside, and no coach explaining expectations. What replaces teammates is coworkers. What replaces coaches is management. And what replaces a clearly defined role is often ambiguity.

For many former players, this transition is more jarring than expected.

Why the Workplace Feels Foreign After Sports

Sports environments are unusually clear.

You know who is in charge.

You know how playing time is earned.

You know what success looks like on the scoreboard.

You know when feedback is coming and where it will come from.

Most workplaces are not built that way.

Authority is layered and indirect.

Performance metrics are vague.

Feedback is inconsistent or nonexistent.

Politics often matter as much as output.

For athletes raised in merit-based systems, this feels disorienting. You are used to competing for spots with effort, preparation, and execution. Suddenly, effort alone does not guarantee progress.

That gap creates frustration, and frustration often leads to stalled careers and unstable income growth.

Authority Without Coaches

In baseball, authority is obvious.

Manager.

Coaching staff.

Veteran leaders.

They tell you where to be, when to be there, and what is expected. If you miss, you hear about it immediately.

In the workplace, authority is often unclear.

Your manager may not control promotions.

Your manager may not give direct feedback.

Your manager may not advocate for you.

Instead of one voice, there are multiple influences. HR. Leadership. Office culture. Unspoken rules.

Former athletes struggle here because they are waiting for coaching that never comes.

You wait to be told how you are doing.

You wait to be told what to fix.

You wait to be told what comes next.

In many workplaces, no one tells you unless something goes wrong.

That silence is not approval. It is ambiguity.

Feedback Without Film

Baseball feedback is immediate and objective.

Film does not lie.

Stats do not lie.

Performance is visible.

You know when you are struggling. You know when you are improving. The numbers and the tape tell the story.

Workplace feedback is often delayed, filtered, or avoided entirely.

You might only hear feedback during annual reviews.

You might get vague comments instead of clear direction.

You might get praise that does not translate into advancement.

This creates a dangerous gap.

Athletes are used to adjusting quickly. Without feedback, you cannot adjust. Without adjustment, growth stalls.

Income growth follows the same pattern.

If you do not know how performance is measured, you cannot optimize it.

If you do not know what leads to promotion, you cannot pursue it intentionally.

You end up working hard in the wrong areas, which feels familiar but produces different results.

Politics, Ambiguity, and Unclear Expectations

This is where many athletes disengage.

In sports, politics exist, but performance eventually wins.

In the workplace, politics often shape opportunity.

Relationships matter. Visibility matters. Timing matters. Sometimes the best performer does not advance.

For former players, this feels unfair and exhausting. You were trained to let performance speak. Now you are expected to advocate for yourself, manage perception, and navigate personalities.

Ignoring this reality does not protect you. It limits you.

Financially, this has consequences.

Slower promotions mean slower income growth.

Unclear roles increase job instability.

Missed opportunities delay savings, investing, and long-term security.

Understanding the game you are in is not selling out. It is adapting.

How This Impacts Income Growth and Career Stability

In baseball, career length depends on performance and availability.

In the workplace, career stability depends on clarity, communication, and positioning.

Athletes who struggle to adapt often experience:

Frequent job changes

Stalled compensation

Underemployment relative to potential

Financial stress despite effort

This is not a work ethic problem. It is a translation problem.

You learned how to compete in one system. Now you must learn how to operate in another.

Income growth is tied to:

Understanding expectations

Communicating value

Building trust with decision-makers

Positioning yourself for opportunity

These are skills, just like hitting or fielding. They can be learned.

Translating Athletic Skills to the Workplace

Former athletes actually have advantages, once they adjust.

You understand preparation.

You understand accountability.

You understand working through slumps.

The mistake is assuming the workplace will recognize those traits automatically.

In baseball, effort is visible.

In the workplace, effort must be translated into outcomes and communicated clearly.

That means:

Asking for feedback instead of waiting

Clarifying expectations early

Documenting wins

Advocating for growth conversations

This is not arrogance. It is professionalism.

Coach's Perspective

A coach would be blunt.

"This isn't the same game."

"Learn the rules or get left behind."

"Effort matters, but awareness matters more."

"Control what you can control."

In baseball, you adjust to pitchers. In work, you adjust to environments.

Complaining about the system does not change it. Learning it gives you leverage.

Game Situations and Decision Points

You are working hard but not advancing.

Do you ask for clarity, or assume effort will eventually be noticed?

You receive vague feedback.

Do you press for specifics, or guess and hope?

You feel frustrated by politics.

Do you disengage, or learn how to navigate them without losing integrity?

Each decision compounds over time.

Common Athlete Mistakes and Financial Parallels

Athletes wait for coaching.

Financially, that delays income growth.

Athletes rely on effort alone.

Financially, that leads to stagnation.

Athletes disengage when systems feel unfair.

Financially, that creates instability.

The workplace is a different league. You still compete, but the scoreboard looks different.

Winning the Long Game

The most successful former athletes do not abandon their identity. They expand it.

They keep their discipline.

They add communication.

They replace assumptions with clarity.

They treat careers like seasons, not games. They make adjustments. They learn from mistakes. They position themselves for longevity.

Income stability is not about one job. It is about understanding how careers actually move.

Athlete Takeaways

- The workplace has different rules. Learn them early.
- Effort matters, but clarity drives advancement.
- Feedback is not automatic. Ask for it.
- Income growth follows positioning, not just performance.
- Adaptation is not weakness. It is professionalism.

Chapter 28: When No One Is Watching Anymore

Every baseball player knows the difference between practice with eyes on you and work done alone.

In-season, everything is monitored.

Weights are scheduled.

Workouts are mandatory.

Film is reviewed.

Lineups are posted.

Accountability is built into the environment. You do not have to manufacture discipline because discipline is enforced.

Then the season ends. Or your playing career ends.

And suddenly, no one is watching.

No coach checks your arrival time.

No strength staff tracks your reps.

No manager posts depth charts.

No film session exposes mistakes.

What remains is freedom. And for many former athletes, that freedom quietly becomes the most dangerous opponent they will ever face.

The Discipline Gap After Accountability Disappears

Athletes are often described as "disciplined," but most discipline in sports is structured discipline.

You did not decide when practice started.

You did not choose whether conditioning happened.

You did not negotiate film sessions.

The system handled that for you.

When the system disappears, the responsibility shifts inward. That transition exposes a gap many athletes do not expect.

Without external accountability, habits weaken.

Without consequences, standards slip.

Without pressure, urgency fades.

This is not laziness. It is adjustment shock.

You were trained to respond to structure, not to build it from scratch.

Why Former Athletes Self-Sabotage Without Pressure

Self-sabotage rarely looks dramatic at first.

It looks like skipping workouts.

It looks like spending instead of saving.

It looks like "I'll start next month."

It looks like comfort replacing urgency.

In sports, pressure keeps you sharp. Games matter. Playing time matters. Mistakes are visible.

In adult life, consequences are delayed.

You can overspend for years before it hurts.

You can neglect saving and feel fine until an emergency hits.

You can drift professionally and still collect a paycheck.

The absence of immediate consequences tricks your brain into thinking nothing is wrong.

That is when standards drop quietly.

Athletes who thrived under pressure often struggle without it because pressure once did the thinking for them.

Comfort vs Growth Decisions

In baseball, you always know which choice is comfortable and which one leads to growth.

Comfort is skipping extra reps.

Growth is staying late.

Comfort is swinging for contact.

Growth is refining mechanics.

After sports, those choices become less obvious, but they still exist.

Comfort looks like lifestyle inflation.

Growth looks like saving when you could spend.

Comfort looks like staying in a job that feels safe.

Growth looks like developing new skills.

Comfort feels earned. Growth feels inconvenient.

Without a coach demanding growth, comfort wins more often than athletes expect.

The danger is not one comfortable decision. It is thousands of them stacked over time.

Translating "Grind Culture" Into Adult Life

Athletes are raised in grind culture.

Early mornings.

Late nights.

No excuses.

Earn everything.

But grind culture without direction becomes burnout.

In sports, grind has a purpose.

There is a season.

There is a goal.

There is recovery.

In adult life, endless grind without structure leads to exhaustion, not progress.

The key is translation, not replication.

Adult discipline is not about doing more.

It is about doing the right things consistently.

That means:

Automating good decisions

Reducing friction

Building systems instead of relying on motivation

In baseball terms, it is less about swinging harder and more about improving plate discipline.

Why Money Mistakes Show Up Years Later

Financial mistakes are delayed penalties.

You do not feel the cost of not saving immediately.

You do not feel the impact of bad debt right away.

You do not feel the consequence of inaction until time passes.

That delay is why athletes get caught off guard.

In sports, mistakes are immediate.

In money, mistakes compound quietly.

Skipping saving in your 20s does not hurt in your 20s.

It hurts in your 40s and 50s.

Ignoring structure early does not create pain early.

It creates regret later.

Former athletes often say, "I wish I had known sooner."

What they usually mean is, "I wish I had kept my standards when no one was watching."

Building Internal Accountability

The most successful former athletes rebuild structure intentionally.

They replace external accountability with internal systems.

Calendars become the new practice schedule.

Automatic savings becomes the new mandatory lift.

Check-ins become the new film sessions.

This is not about motivation. Motivation fades.

This is about systems.

Systems run when discipline is low.

Systems protect you from yourself.

The goal is not to be perfect.

The goal is to make the right behavior the default.

Coach's Perspective

A coach would not soften this.

"No one cares now. That's reality."

"Standards don't disappear just because oversight does."

"Who you are when no one's watching matters most."

"Discipline is doing the work without applause."

In sports, character is revealed under pressure.

In life, character is revealed in silence.

Game Situations and Decision Points

You get paid. No one tells you what to do with it.

Do you protect future you, or reward present you?

You have free time. No workout is scheduled.

Do you move your body, or stay comfortable?

You have no financial emergency yet.

Do you prepare anyway, or assume you'll handle it later?

These are quiet moments. They define outcomes.

Common Athlete Mistakes and Financial Parallels

Athletes relax standards after structure disappears.

Financially, that leads to drift.

Athletes mistake comfort for recovery.

Financially, that leads to lifestyle creep.

Athletes rely on intensity instead of systems.

Financially, that leads to inconsistency.

What once made you elite can work against you if not adapted.

Winning the Long Game

The athletes who thrive long after sports are not the ones who grind the hardest.

They are the ones who rebuild structure.

They set rules for themselves.

They automate discipline.

They protect their future without needing pressure.

They understand that nobody watching is not an excuse. It is a test.

The season does not end when the uniform comes off. It changes.

Athlete Takeaways

- Discipline without structure fades fast. Build your own system.
- Comfort feels good now. Growth pays off later.
- Grind culture must evolve into sustainable habits.
- Money mistakes are delayed penalties. Prepare early.
- Who you are when no one is watching determines the outcome.

Chapter 29: Redefining Winning After the Uniform Comes Off

Every baseball player remembers the first time the game stopped defining their identity.

Maybe it was the day you cleaned out your locker.

Maybe it was the first spring without reporting to camp.

Maybe it was when someone asked, "So what do you do now?" and you hesitated.

For years, winning had a clear definition.

Wins and losses.

Stats and standings.

Roster spots and contracts.

The scoreboard told you exactly where you stood.

Then the uniform comes off, and the scoreboard disappears.

No box score.

No rankings.

No coach telling you whether you played well enough.

That absence creates confusion. And when clarity disappears, people default to substitutes.

Why Chasing Status Replaces Chasing Performance

In sports, performance is visible.

You either produced or you did not.

You either earned playing time or you did not.

After sports, performance becomes harder to measure. Effort is less visible. Progress is slower. Feedback is vague. That vacuum creates an opening for status to take over.

Status is easier to see than fulfillment.

Titles.

Income.

Houses.

Cars.

Lifestyle.

These become proxy scoreboards. They are external, visible, and comparable.

The problem is that status looks like winning without guaranteeing it feels like winning.

Many former athletes chase status because it resembles the old validation system. It gives quick feedback. It tells a story to the outside world. It replaces the applause that disappeared.

But status is a weak substitute for purpose.

Income vs Fulfillment

Income matters. Pretending it does not is dishonest.

Money creates stability.

It buys options.

It reduces stress.

But income alone does not equal success.

Many former athletes reach income goals and still feel restless. The number goes up, but satisfaction does not. That disconnect creates confusion.

In baseball terms, this is like chasing contract size while ignoring role fit, health, or longevity.

Fulfillment comes from alignment.

Alignment between effort and values.

Alignment between time spent and meaning created.

Alignment between who you are and how you live.

Income supports fulfillment. It does not replace it.

When income becomes the only scoreboard, people sacrifice health, relationships, and peace without realizing it until much later.

Titles, Houses, Cars, and Comparison Traps

Comparison is unavoidable. Social media turned it into a full-time sport.

Former teammates show promotions.

Friends show homes.

People your age show milestones.

The trap is assuming these visible markers represent happiness, security, or success.

Titles do not reveal stress.

Houses do not show debt.

Cars do not show anxiety.

In baseball, you knew better than to judge players by batting practice highlights. You understood context. You understood roles. You understood timing.

Money requires the same awareness.

Comparison pulls people out of their own game plan. It pushes them to chase milestones that do not fit their life, income stability, or values.

That is how people win someone else's game and lose their own.

What Success Actually Looks Like in Your 30s and 40s

Success evolves.

In your playing days, success meant opportunity. Making the team. Staying healthy. Competing.

In your 30s and 40s, success looks different.

Control over your time.

Stability without constant stress.

Health that supports longevity.

Relationships that are not neglected.

Financial systems that run quietly in the background.

Success is less about upside and more about sustainability.

In baseball terms, this is moving from chasing raw power to mastering situational hitting. You stop trying to impress and start trying to win the inning.

People who redefine success early build lives that last. People who do not keep chasing applause long after the crowd has moved on.

Building a New Scoreboard

You need a new way to measure winning.

Not one handed to you. One you choose intentionally.

A healthy scoreboard includes things like:

Consistency instead of intensity

Progress instead of perfection

Alignment instead of appearance

It asks better questions.

Do my financial decisions reduce stress or create it?

Does my work support the life I want, or crowd it out?

Am I building options, or just obligations?

This scoreboard is quieter. It does not trend online. It does not impress strangers.

But it works.

The Identity Shift Former Athletes Resist

The hardest part of redefining winning is letting go of the old identity.

Athletes are conditioned to tie self-worth to performance. When that performance ends, the identity wobbles.

Some people respond by chasing louder wins.

Others withdraw entirely.

The healthiest path is integration.

You are not your sport.

But your sport shaped you.

The discipline, resilience, and work ethic still matter. They just apply to different arenas.

Winning now is about building a life that holds up without a scoreboard watching.

Coach's Perspective

A coach would not sugarcoat this.

"Nobody's clapping anymore. That's real life."

"Stop playing for approval."

"Know what winning actually looks like now."

"Build something that lasts."

"Do not confuse noise with progress."

In sports, maturity shows when players stop forcing highlights. In life, maturity shows when people stop chasing validation.

Game Situations and Decision Points

You get a promotion with higher pay and worse hours.

Do you chase the title or protect your balance?

You can afford a bigger lifestyle upgrade.

Do you buy it because it fits your values or because others will see it?

You feel behind compared to peers.

Do you adjust your plan or abandon it?

These decisions are not dramatic. They are cumulative.

Common Athlete Mistakes and Financial Parallels

Athletes chase recognition instead of mastery.

Financially, that shows up as lifestyle inflation.

Athletes equate effort with worth.

Financially, that leads to burnout chasing numbers.

Athletes resist identity evolution.

Financially, that leads to rigid, outdated goals.

Growth requires redefining success, not doubling down on old definitions.

Winning the Long Game

Winning after sports is quieter.

It looks like stability.

It looks like flexibility.

It looks like waking up without dread.

The athletes who win long-term are not the loudest. They are the most aligned.

They stop chasing the old scoreboard.

They build a new one.

They play their game, not everyone else's.

That is real winning.

Athlete Takeaways

- Status is not the same as success. Do not confuse them.
- Income supports fulfillment but does not replace it.
- Comparison pulls you out of your own game plan.
- Success evolves. Adjust your scoreboard accordingly.
- Real winning is building a life that holds up without applause.

Chapter 30: Staying Connected Without Living in the Past

Every baseball player knows the feeling of walking into a clubhouse.

The smell of the grass.

The noise.

The rhythm of the day already set for you.

You know where to be, when to be there, and who you belong with. Even on hard days, you are surrounded by people who understand the grind without explanation.

Then one day, the clubhouse is gone.

No team-issued schedule.

No built-in community.

No automatic locker room.

That absence hits harder than most former athletes expect.

The Role of Community, Mentorship, and New Locker Rooms

Sports solve a problem most adults struggle with. They give you instant community.

You do not have to search for it. You are drafted into it. You earn your place through effort, and the bond forms through shared work, shared failure, and shared pressure.

After sports, that structure disappears. And many former athletes underestimate how important it was.

Community is not optional. It is foundational.

Without it, discipline erodes. Motivation fades. Perspective narrows. When no one sees your effort and no one expects your presence, it becomes easier to drift.

Mentorship fills a similar role.

Coaches once corrected you in real time. Veterans showed you how to prepare. Leaders modeled behavior. After sports, many people stop receiving feedback entirely.

That silence is dangerous.

New locker rooms do not look like the old ones. They are not loud. They are not automatic. But they matter just as much.

They might be:

- A group of peers in your profession
- A training group or gym community
- A mastermind or accountability circle
- A purpose-driven organization or cause

The form changes. The need does not.

Why Isolation Hits Former Athletes Hard

Isolation does not arrive dramatically. It creeps in quietly.

Schedules loosen.

Conversations become surface-level.

Work becomes transactional.

Former athletes often go from being surrounded daily to operating alone without realizing the impact.

The loss is not just social. It is structural.

Teams provide accountability.

They provide identity reinforcement.

They provide shared language and struggle.

Without those elements, many former athletes experience:

- Loss of motivation
- Difficulty maintaining routines
- Emotional flatness or restlessness
- Increased financial mistakes due to stress or boredom

Isolation makes discipline harder because discipline thrives in community.

In baseball terms, this is trying to stay sharp without teammates pushing you in practice. You can do it, but it is much harder and most people do not.

Finding Purpose Without the Team

Purpose used to be obvious.

Win today.

Prepare for tomorrow.

Help the team.

After sports, purpose becomes abstract. No one assigns it. No one measures it for you.

Many former athletes mistake productivity for purpose. They stay busy but feel empty. Others mistake nostalgia for meaning and get stuck reliving past seasons.

Purpose now must be chosen.

It often comes from:

- Contribution rather than competition
- Impact rather than recognition
- Growth rather than validation

This shift is uncomfortable because it lacks instant feedback.

In baseball terms, it is the transition from chasing stats to mentoring younger players. The satisfaction is deeper, but quieter.

Purpose without the team is less about winning and more about building.

Healthy Nostalgia vs Being Stuck

Nostalgia is not the enemy.

Remembering good seasons, great teammates, and meaningful moments is healthy. Those memories shaped you. They matter.

The problem arises when nostalgia becomes a substitute for growth.

Healthy nostalgia:

- Honors the past without living in it
- Extracts lessons and values
- Inspires forward movement

Being stuck looks different:

- Constantly comparing the present to the past
- Measuring current life against former glory
- Avoiding new challenges because they lack familiarity

In baseball terms, this is the veteran who only talks about old stats and never adapts to the new role.

The past should inform you, not trap you.

Creating a Forward-Looking Identity

Identity does not disappear when sports end. It evolves.

Former athletes often struggle because their identity was externally reinforced. Jerseys, titles, and roles made it visible. Without those signals, uncertainty creeps in.

A forward-looking identity answers new questions:

- Who am I becoming, not who was I?
- What values carry forward regardless of setting?
- How do I want to show up when no one is watching?

This identity is quieter. It is internal. It is less fragile.

It is built through:

- Consistent routines
- Meaningful work
- Intentional relationships
- Long-term financial discipline

You stop needing applause to feel progress.

That is maturity.

Mentorship as a Two-Way Street

Many former athletes think mentorship only flows downward.

That is incomplete.

You still need mentors. People ahead of you in career, life, and financial wisdom. But you also need to mentor others.

Teaching reinforces discipline.

Leading restores purpose.

Giving perspective sharpens your own.

In baseball, leadership often emerges late in a career. The same is true in life.

Mentorship reconnects you to community without trapping you in the past.

Coach's Perspective

A coach would be direct.

"Don't isolate."

"Find your people."

"Be part of something."

"Honor the past, but don't live there."

"Build your next locker room."

No coach would let a player train alone indefinitely. Life deserves the same structure.

Game Situations and Decision Points

You feel disconnected from your current work.

Do you withdraw or seek new community?

You miss the team environment.

Do you relive it or recreate it in a new form?

You are proud of your past.

Do you let it define you or support what comes next?

These are not emotional decisions. They are strategic ones.

Common Athlete Mistakes and Financial Parallels

Athletes isolate after competition ends.

Financially, that leads to unexamined habits.

Athletes cling to identity.

Financially, that leads to outdated goals.

Athletes avoid new locker rooms.

Financially, that leads to stagnation.

Connection keeps systems alive.

Winning the Long Game

You do not need to forget who you were.

You need to expand who you are.

The athletes who thrive after sports build new communities, seek mentorship, and stay connected without being anchored to the past.

They respect the game they played without letting it be the last chapter.

They stay in the game by evolving.

Athlete Takeaways

- Community is not optional. Build new locker rooms intentionally.
- Isolation erodes discipline faster than failure.
- Honor the past without living in it.
- Purpose now comes from contribution, not competition.
- Stay connected, stay growing, and keep moving forward.

Glossary of Baseball and Financial Terms

This glossary connects key financial concepts to familiar ideas from baseball, making money easier to understand through the language, structure, and discipline players already know.

Asset Allocation

Financial Definition:

How money is divided among different investment types such as stocks, bonds, and cash to balance risk and return.

Baseball Comparison:

How playing time, roles, and responsibilities are distributed across the lineup and pitching staff. Too much reliance on one position or one arm without balance creates exposure over a long season.

Assets

Financial Definition:

Things you own that have value, such as cash, investments, real estate, or retirement accounts.

Baseball Comparison:

Your tools as a player. Bat speed, arm strength, instincts, conditioning, and experience that contribute to overall performance.

Bonds

Financial Definition:

Loans made to governments or companies that pay interest and return principal over time.

Baseball Comparison:

Solid defense and reliable pitching. Not flashy, but essential for controlling games when pressure rises.

Budget

Financial Definition:

A plan for how income is allocated toward expenses, savings, and goals.

Baseball Comparison:

The game plan. If you do not know when to bunt, take a pitch, or swing away, execution breaks down.

Cash Flow

Financial Definition:

Money coming in versus money going out.

Baseball Comparison:

Stamina across innings. If you burn energy early without control, you struggle late.

Compounding

Financial Definition:

Earnings that generate additional earnings over time.

Baseball Comparison:

Daily reps and routine. One good swing does not matter. Thousands over time change your career.

Credit

Financial Definition:

The ability to borrow money with the promise of repayment.

Baseball Comparison:

Trust from the coaching staff. Earned through consistency, lost quickly through mistakes.

Debt

Financial Definition:

Money borrowed that must be repaid, often with interest.

Baseball Comparison:

Extra weight or injury risk. Manageable when intentional, damaging when ignored.

Diversification

Financial Definition:

Spreading investments across different assets to reduce risk.

Baseball Comparison:

Building a complete roster instead of relying on one superstar to carry the season.

Emergency Fund

Financial Definition:

Savings set aside for unexpected expenses.

Baseball Comparison:

Depth on the bench. You hope you never need it, but it saves seasons when something goes wrong.

ETF (Exchange-Traded Fund)

Financial Definition:

A fund that holds many investments and trades like a stock.

Baseball Comparison:

A team-first approach instead of a solo effort.

Fees and Expense Ratios

Financial Definition:

Costs associated with managing investments.

Baseball Comparison:

Mental errors. One may not cost you the game, but repeated mistakes lose seasons.

Growth Investing

Financial Definition:

Investing in companies expected to grow faster than average.

Baseball Comparison:

Swinging for extra bases. Higher upside, but requires strong fundamentals.

Insurance

Financial Definition:

Protection against financial loss from unexpected events.

Baseball Comparison:

Protective gear. You do not step into the box without it when risk increases.

Liquidity

Financial Definition:

How easily money can be accessed without penalty or delay.

Baseball Comparison:

Flexibility late in the game. The ability to adjust without forcing bad decisions.

Net Worth

Financial Definition:

Assets minus liabilities.

Baseball Comparison:

The full season stat line. Not one at-bat, but the total outcome.

Rebalancing

Financial Definition:

Adjusting investments back to their intended mix over time.

Baseball Comparison:

Mid-season adjustments to keep performance steady and prevent fatigue or overuse.

Risk

Financial Definition:

The chance that outcomes differ from expectations, including loss.

Baseball Comparison:

Pitch selection. Higher reward comes with higher risk if poorly timed.

Roth IRA

Financial Definition:

A retirement account where money grows tax-free if rules are followed.

Baseball Comparison:

Early discipline so the ninth inning is easier to close.

Stocks

Financial Definition:

Ownership shares in a company.

Baseball Comparison:

Everyday position players. They drive offense but need support to win consistently.

Tax-Advantaged Accounts

Financial Definition:

Accounts that provide tax benefits, often with rules and restrictions.

Baseball Comparison:

League rules. Restrictions exist to protect fairness and long-term success.

Volatility

Financial Definition:

Short-term ups and downs in market value.

Baseball Comparison:

Slumps. Normal part of the season unless you panic and abandon fundamentals.

Permanent Loss

Financial Definition:

Money that cannot recover due to poor decisions or panic.

Baseball Comparison:

An avoidable error. Usually caused by rushing or ignoring fundamentals.

Total Return

Financial Definition:

Investment return from both price growth and income.

Baseball Comparison:

Runs, defense, and pitching combined. Every phase matters.

Value Investing

Financial Definition:

Investing in assets believed to be undervalued.

Baseball Comparison:

Clean execution. Not flashy, but wins consistently.

Yield

Financial Definition:

Income generated from an investment.

Baseball Comparison:

Consistent run production. Not dramatic, but reliable.

Final Note

This glossary reinforces one core principle:

Financial success, like success in baseball, comes from balance, discipline, timing, and repetition.

That philosophy runs throughout **Baseball Money 101** and continues long after the final out.

Disclaimers

Educational Purpose Only

This book is for educational purposes only.

The information provided in **Baseball Money 101** is intended to help readers understand general financial concepts using baseball-based analogies. It is not individualized financial, investment, tax, legal, or insurance advice.

Every financial situation is different. Your goals, income, family circumstances, risk tolerance, and time horizon are unique. What works for one person may not be appropriate for another.

Not Financial, Investment, or Legal Advice

Nothing in this book should be interpreted as a recommendation to buy, sell, or hold any specific investment, financial product, or strategy.

This book does not replace advice from qualified professionals such as:

- Financial advisors
- Accountants or tax professionals
- Attorneys
- Insurance professionals

Before making financial decisions, readers should consult professionals who can evaluate their individual situation.

No Guarantees or Promises of Results

All investing involves risk, including the possible loss of principal.

Past performance does not guarantee future results. Markets fluctuate. Economic conditions change. Outcomes cannot be predicted or guaranteed.

The examples and scenarios in this book are illustrative only and may not reflect actual results or real-world outcomes.

Tax and Legal Information

Any discussion of taxes, retirement accounts, estate planning, or legal structures is general in nature.

Tax laws and regulations change frequently and vary by jurisdiction. Legal requirements differ based on location and personal circumstances. Readers should seek personalized tax or legal advice before acting on any information related to these topics.

Athlete and Career Considerations

This book discusses financial topics as they relate to athletes and former athletes, including career transitions, income variability, and life after competition.

It does not provide career placement services, employment advice, or guarantees related to income, compensation, or career success.

Use of Analogies

Baseball and sports analogies are used throughout this book to make financial concepts easier to understand.

These analogies are educational tools only and should not be interpreted literally. Financial decisions require analysis beyond analogy and should be based on personal circumstances, professional guidance, and sound judgment.

Personal Responsibility

By reading this book, you acknowledge that:

- You are responsible for your own financial decisions
- You understand that financial outcomes involve uncertainty
- You agree to seek appropriate professional guidance when needed

Education improves decision-making, but responsibility remains with the individual.

Contact Information

If you would like to learn more about the concepts discussed in this book or explore additional educational resources, Pat Brown can be found through public platforms including LinkedIn, Twitter, and via Google search.

For questions specifically related to **Baseball Money 101**, you may contact Pat Brown at:

info@baseballmoney101.com

Final Reminder

Financial success is built over time through discipline, planning, and consistency.

This book provides a framework, not a guarantee.

Use it as a guide, not a substitute for professional advice.

Pat Brown OLB, University of Kansas

Made in the USA
Monee, IL
04 November 2026

67387593R00138